insight text guide

Virginia Lee

All About Eve

Dir. Joseph Mankiewicz

First published in 2013, reprinted in 2014, 2015 (twice), 2017 (twice).

Insight Publications Pty Ltd
3/350 Charman Road
Cheltenham VIC 3192
Australia
Tel: +61 3 8571 4950
Fax: +61 3 8571 0257
Email: books@insightpublications.com.au

www.insightpublications.com.au

National Library of Australia Cataloguing-in-Publication entry:
Lee, Virginia, author.
Joseph Mankiewicz's All about Eve / Virginia Lee.
9781922243119 (paperback)
Insight text guide.
Includes bibliographical references.
For secondary school age.
Mankiewicz, Joseph L.—Criticism and interpretation.
All about Eve (Motion picture)
791.4372

Other ISBNs:
9781925175011 (digital)
9781925175349 (bundle: print + digital)

Cover design: The Modern Art Production Group

Printed in Australia.

contents

CHARACTER MAP

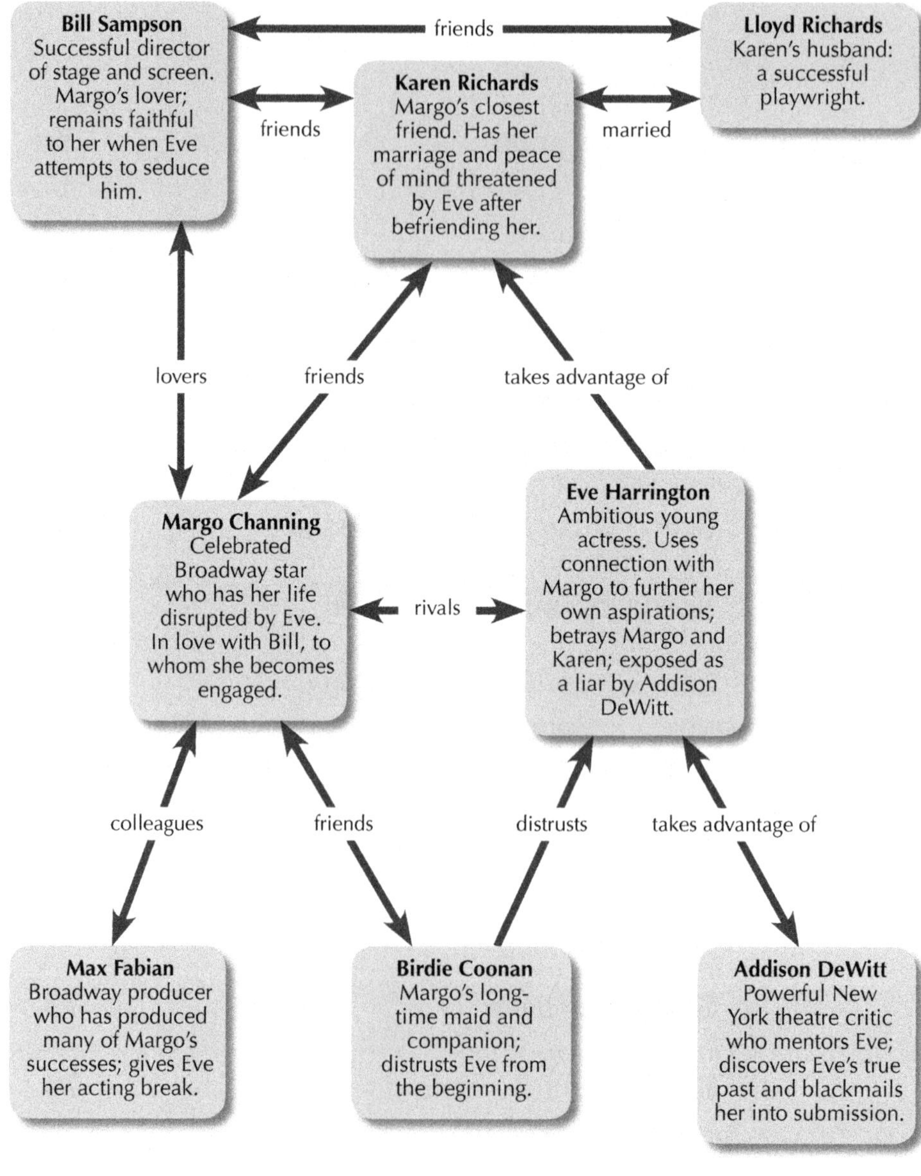

OVERVIEW

About the director

Joseph L. Mankiewicz (1909–1993) was a successful American film director, screenwriter and producer; he is still the only director to have won back-to-back Oscars for both direction and screenwriting. Mankiewicz first went to Hollywood as a young man to join his older brother Herman, who was also a distinguished screenwriter (he wrote *Citizen Kane*). Joseph Mankiewicz's eclectic Hollywood career encompassed a wide variety of genres – from the incisive social commentary of *A Letter to Three Wives* (1949), to the musical *Guys and Dolls* (1955), the sombre drama of *Suddenly Last Summer* (1959) and the extravagant historical epic of *Cleopatra* (1963). His last film, *Sleuth*, was made in 1972.

All About Eve (1950) was written and directed by Mankiewicz and is generally regarded as his finest film. Critically praised and commercially successful at the time of its release, it has endured as a classic of American cinema. It was nominated for fourteen Academy Awards and won six, including Best Picture. Of particular note was the fact that it received four female acting nominations, cementing Mankiewicz's reputation as a brilliant writer of complex, multi-dimensional roles for women. Many of Mankiewicz's key concerns – the idea of the theatre as a societal metaphor, the masks people adopt, dynamics within male–female relationships and the ways in which ambition corrupts – are explored in *All About Eve*. The film also demonstrates Mankiewicz's interest in revisiting and reappraising the past, often using a flashback narration, which became one of his signature techniques.

After working in Hollywood for many years, Mankiewicz became increasingly disillusioned with the political conservatism of the film industry, ultimately relocating to New York to found his own independent production company.

Synopsis

As Eve Harrington, Broadway's newest star, is honoured with acting's most prestigious award at the annual Sarah Siddons Society dinner, various theatrical personalities witness the ceremony. They include director Bill Sampson, playwright Lloyd Richards and his wife Karen, star of the stage Margo Channing and theatre critic Addison DeWitt. DeWitt muses on Eve's remarkable rise to celebrity, but it is clear not all her colleagues approve of the young actress.

Karen Richards, Margo's closest friend, then describes her first meeting with Eve, eight months before, and for the remainder of the film the events unfold from this flashback. As the long flashback begins, Karen is approached by Eve outside the theatre where Margo's play, *Aged in Wood*, is being performed. Eve presents herself as a devoted fan of Margo's and Karen decides the two must meet. After hearing Eve's sad history, Margo offers friendship and employment to the young woman.

Margo is initially delighted with her new personal assistant. However, she becomes concerned after her friend and employee Birdie expresses her mistrust of Eve, and soon Eve's efficiency and unfailing desire to please start to grate. Margo's insecurities rise to the surface and she suspects Eve of having designs on her lover, Bill. Things come to a head the night of Bill's welcome-home party. Margo becomes drunk and abusive, arguing with Bill and the Richardses, as well as targeting Eve. However, before retiring to bed in a maudlin huff, she asks her friend, producer Max Fabian, to give Eve a job. In the meantime, Eve harbours other plans and solicits Karen's influence to help her secure a position as Margo's understudy.

Max has also promised Claudia Casswell, Addison DeWitt's latest protégé, an audition for a small part in *Aged in Wood* and Margo has agreed to read with her. But Margo arrives late and Eve, as Margo's understudy, reads instead, dazzling Bill, Lloyd and Addison. Margo, furious, dismisses Eve's explanations, fights with Lloyd and accuses Bill of being more than professionally interested in her former employee. Bill cannot allay her fears and, with regret, breaks off their relationship.

Later, after listening to the still-angry Lloyd, Karen decides that Margo needs a lesson. She phones Eve to alert her that she may have to step in as Margo's understudy sooner rather than later. The Richardses and Margo go away for the weekend and, unbeknown to Lloyd, Karen empties the fuel tank, impeding their journey home. Margo misses the play and Eve gives a memorable performance in her stead. Eve herself had notified a number of critics of the change in casting and, subsequently, Addison writes a spiteful review, praising Eve and disparaging Margo. Eve's hypocrisy and her underlying agenda are now clear to Karen. Bill, who has been propositioned by Eve, also recognises her duplicity and returns to comfort the devastated Margo. Foolishly, Lloyd continues to make excuses for Eve.

The Richardses join Margo and Bill for dinner where the latter couple announce their decision to marry. Coincidentally, Addison and Eve are together at the same restaurant. In the ladies' room, Eve blackmails Karen, threatening to tell Margo of Karen's ruse unless she is given the part of Cora in Lloyd's new play. Shaken, Karen returns to the others and, with great relief, welcomes Margo's unexpected announcement that she no longer wants the role.

Eve does get the part, but rehearsals for *Footsteps on the Ceiling* are volatile and stressful, with Bill and Lloyd arguing bitterly. Karen fears that Lloyd is attracted to Eve. The night before the play premieres off Broadway, Addison confronts Eve in her hotel room. He makes it clear that he expects to be her lover and when she tells him that she intends to marry Lloyd, he blackmails her. Addison has discovered the truth about Eve's past and will hold it over her head. The show opens and Eve gives 'the performance of her life'.

This phrase returns the narrative to the Siddons banquet. Eve accepts her award, receives cursory congratulations from the Richardses, Margo and Bill, but refuses to go to the party being held in her honour. Back at her apartment, she is surprised by a young woman, Phoebe, who slipped in while the maid wasn't watching. Phoebe is a fan with aspirations of her own; the cycle is about to start again.

Character summaries

Margo Channing

The protagonist of *All About Eve*. Margo is a famous stage actress; forty years old. Close friends with Karen Richards; romantically involved with Bill Sampson. Offers Eve Harrington a job and a place to stay.

Eve Harrington

The antagonist (anti-hero) of the film. Approximately twenty-four years old; fan of Margo Channing's and would-be actress; manipulates her way into Margo's life as her personal assistant; becomes her understudy and, finally, her rival. Threatens Margo's personal relationships.

Karen Richards

Margo's closest friend and confidante; in her mid-thirties. Married to playwright Lloyd Richards. Introduces Eve to Margo and, initially, is supportive of her aspirations.

Lloyd Richards

Successful playwright who has written many of Margo's roles. In his late thirties; married to Karen; close friends with Margo and Bill. Taken in by Eve's apparent sincerity.

Bill Sampson

Rising director of both theatre and film; thirty-two years old. Close friends with the Richardses; in love with Margo; finally persuades her to marry him. Rejects Eve when she tries to seduce him.

Addison DeWitt

Influential New York theatre critic; in his mid-forties; moves in the same theatrical circle as Margo and her friends. Recognises Eve's talent; exposes her lies and seeks to control her career.

Max Fabian

Successful Broadway producer; about sixty. Has produced many of Margo's theatrical successes; produces *Footsteps on the Ceiling,* the play that brings Eve her fame.

Birdie Coonan

Margo's devoted friend and employee; about fifty; old vaudevillian performer. Mistrusts Eve from the outset.

Claudia Casswell

Addison's protégé; early twenties; wants to be an actress.

Phoebe

Another ambitious young woman who wants to act; fan of Eve's; sneaks into her apartment to effect a meeting.

BACKGROUND & CONTEXT

Golden Age of Hollywood

The period in which *All About Eve* was made is often called the 'Golden Age of Hollywood'. From the advent of 'talkies' (the first films with soundtracks) in the late 1920s, to the early 1960s, the film industry was dominated by the studio system. Major studios such as Twentieth Century Fox employed thousands of actors, directors, writers, technicians and other staff under contract, thereby controlling their labour and professional practice. By the mid-1940s, at the height of the industry's popularity, the studios were producing over four hundred films a year to worldwide audiences, hungry for entertainment. These films were characterised by a commitment to realism; clearly defined characters; a strong, linear plot-line, unambiguously resolved; and an increasingly moralistic tone. By the 1960s though, the studio system was in decline. The influence of foreign films and the emergence of independent production companies, as well as the rise of television, all challenged the big studios' monopoly of the film industry.

All About Eve was based on a short story, *The Wisdom of Eve*, by Mary Orr, first published in *Cosmopolitan* magazine in 1946. However, Mankiewicz's screenplay makes substantial changes – expanding the original narrative, recalibrating the characters and altering the ending – so that the final product bears little resemblance to its source material. The result is widely regarded as one of the most superb films to come out of this classic period of Hollywood cinema.

America in 1950

The film is set only five years after the end of the most devastating war in history. Over 400,000 American servicemen and servicewomen were killed in World War II and, in 1950, their loss would have been a raw and recent memory. Addison's accusation that Eve's invention of a dead husband is 'an insult to dead heroes and the women who loved them' would have resonated with the film's first audiences. It makes Eve into even more of a villain – she is not just a liar, but an insensitive liar.

After such national loss, postwar America was entering into a period of unprecedented economic prosperity. It was a time of fiscal growth, increased consumerism, advertising and selling. Employment opportunities were extensive and the film industry was booming.

Politically, the 1950s was a deeply conservative decade, dominated by the Cold War and the pervasive fear of communism. The House of Un-American Activities Committee (HUAC) had been established in 1938 to counter the communist 'menace'. After World War II, this Committee was determined to flush out and vilify those who 'threatened' the American way of life. This had direct and damaging implications for Hollywood, as writers, directors and actors who were seen to have communist affiliations were targeted by HUAC. Hollywood was bitterly divided between right-wingers testifying against friends and colleagues, and those who opposed such behaviour. As the President of the Screen Directors' Guild, Joseph Mankiewicz belonged to the latter group.

All About Eve is set two decades before the women's liberation movement and there is a pivotal debate running through the film with regard to women's roles. In the 1950s, gender roles were clearly delineated. Women of this generation were largely dependent on men, economically and socially; indeed, many married women were legally required to give up the jobs they had before marriage. Few women went on to further study after school or had ambitions beyond marriage. In the text, Karen's Radcliffe degree does not translate into a career; instead she paints part-time as a hobby. The expectation was that women become homemakers and support their husbands' career aspirations, irrespective of whether they had children.

The Production Code

Hollywood's profound cultural influence both mirrored and reinforced conservative societal standards. From 1930 to 1968, the film industry was regulated by the Production Code, which was initially voluntary and later enforced by an administrating body that saw itself as a moral watchdog, acting as a custodian of public decency. Nudity, overt violence and obscene language were prohibited in motion pictures. Sexuality was rigorously sanitised. In the text, for example, Karen and Lloyd Richards do not share a marital bed, but sleep in modest singles. This coy image was the norm in film and, later, television. The only sex that was depicted on screen was heterosexual, usually featuring nothing more than a chaste kiss.

Like every other Hollywood script, *All About Eve* was scrutinised by the office of the Production Code Administration before the film went into production and Mankiewicz was required to make a number of reluctant cuts to his edgy, at times suggestive, dialogue. Furthermore, given that the Production Code's stated rationale was to protect moral values and attitudes, all filmmakers were constrained by its prescriptive 'working principles' that insisted that good and evil had to be presented in a value-laden way. Accordingly, a character like Eve could not appear too attractive or elicit undue audience sympathy, but had to be punished for transgressing the code of ethical behaviour.

Since the film was made, there has been ongoing speculation as to Eve's sexuality. Conjecture that she may be a lesbian has been based essentially on two scenes. The first is when she walks up the stairs to her apartment with her arm around a young woman who telephones Lloyd in the middle of the night and describes herself (perhaps unreliably) as 'room[ing] across the hall' from Eve. The second is when she implies to Phoebe that she should stay the night. Although neither is conclusive, these scenes are pointed and intriguing. However, given the conservative context in which the film was made, Eve's sexuality – as well as that of the inscrutable Addison DeWitt – can only be inferred.

Broadway

Broadway is still considered the theatrical mecca. Competition is intense and commercial success far from guaranteed. Essentially, little has changed on Broadway since 1950 in terms of the arc of a new play or musical. By the time a show arrives in New York, it is expected to be as honed and polished as possible. New York critics are notoriously harsh and their endorsement is crucial for any new venture to prosper. Productions that represent a significant financial investment can literally close in a week without having reached more than a very small audience. Traditionally, therefore, new productions have always first opened 'off Broadway'. Opening in a smaller theatre, usually in another city altogether, affords the opportunity to gauge public response and make any necessary changes to the show or cast before it hits the 'Big Apple'. This is why Lloyd Richards' new play, *Footsteps on the Ceiling*, opens in New Haven, Connecticut, for a short trial run before coming to Broadway.

Sarah Siddons

Sarah Siddons (1755–1831) was the most celebrated and successful English actress of the eighteenth century. She came from a noted theatrical family, the Kembles, and made her stage debut at an early age. Beautiful, talented and charismatic, she toured the provinces before becoming a star in London at Drury Lane and Covent Garden. Siddons specialised in tragedy and was famous for her Shakespearean roles; in particular, her Lady Macbeth was considered the definitive interpretation. English writer William Hazlitt called her 'tragedy personified' and her portrait was painted several times by the most famous artists of the day, including Sir Joshua Reynolds. Sarah Siddons retired from the stage in 1812.

For the purposes of the film, Mankiewicz invented the Sarah Siddons Award for Distinguished Achievement in the Theatre that is presented to Eve Harrington. The statuette is modelled on Reynolds' famous portrait depicting Siddons as the 'tragic muse', a copy of which hangs in Margo's house. Two years after the film's release, in a case of life imitating art, a real award was initiated by Chicago theatregoers, to be offered annually to honour women's achievements in the theatre. Recipients of this award have included Bette Davis and Celeste Holm.

GENRE, STRUCTURE & LANGUAGE

Genre

All About Eve belongs to the long-established tradition of 'show biz' films that go behind the scenes and explore the drama backstage. The film is both a celebration of the theatre and a critique of the more negative elements – ego, ambition and the ruthless pursuit of fame. *All About Eve* is primarily a drama, but it also has elements of mystery and romance.

Eve's ascent towards stardom is paralleled by the unravelling of her personal relationships, and here we see the elements of romance. Margo and Bill's relationship and the Richardses' marriage are each threatened by Eve's designs. Potentially, there are two romantic triangles. However, both Bill and Lloyd remain faithful to their respective partners and the risk that Eve poses is averted.

The film is also in part a morality fable. In keeping with the didactic (instructive) entertainment style audiences of the 1950s expected, Eve is punished for her duplicity. Her rise to fame carries a hefty price tag and the final view of her, without her friends and with only a drink, a cigarette and the ambiguous Phoebe for company, warns of the dangers of unchecked ambition. Furthermore, the clear parallels between Phoebe and Eve, and the eerie sense that a similar story is about to recur, reinforce the notion of justice being served.

Finally, Mankiewicz's screenplay is, at times, extremely funny. Unusually for films of the period, the humour is verbal and character-driven, rather than situational or slapstick. Some of the lines – for example, Margo's advice to 'Fasten your seatbelts. It's going to be a bumpy night' – have become established catchphrases.

Structure

All About Eve has a circular structure, within which the narrative follows a linear trajectory. The film commences in June, 1950: Eve is about to be presented with the Sarah Siddons award. An extended flashback then takes the audience back to the previous October. We follow Eve's rise from obscurity to stardom, before returning full circle to the moment when Eve collects her award. The film concludes with a short coda, or postscript, that follows Eve home to her apartment that same night. This structure enables us to retrospectively explore Eve's story.

The main plot-line deals with Eve's climb to success and the moral reckoning that shadows it, but there are a number of interconnected subplots: Margo's midlife crisis, Bill and Margo's relationship, the threat to Margo and Karen's friendship, Claudia Casswell's attempts to break into acting, Addison's intervention in Eve's career, and Eve and Lloyd's 'affair'. These issues have all been resolved by the Siddons banquet when the ensemble cast, with the presumed exception of Eve herself, return contentedly to their previous lives.

Language

Mankiewicz's literate, witty screenplay, 'a story for grown-ups' (a phrase used by Margo, Chapter 10), has been called one of the best to come out of Hollywood. It features fast-paced dialogue, sharp observational humour, double entendres, intertextual references and some memorable one-liners. The film's dry, sophisticated tone is established at the outset by Addison. His satirical surveillance of the awards ceremony highlights the unavoidable prevalence of ego in the theatrical profession, and he has this to say on the verbosity of the Master of Ceremonies: 'Being an actor, he will go on speaking for some time'. Addison also makes a sly dig at the theatre's skewed priorities and the traditionally low esteem in which writers are held: 'Minor awards are for such as the writer and director – since their function is merely to construct a tower so that the world can applaud a light which flashes on top of it'.

All About Eve references a number of other texts: for example, Shakespeare's *Macbeth* and *Julius Caesar*, as well as the Bible. These references link back to the characters or the themes, providing an artful commentary on the interactions taking place. Characters themselves often allude to various writers and theatrical personalities. The intertextuality celebrates the talent and creativity of the theatre.

Narrative point of view

All About Eve is anchored by Addison's sardonic voiceover, but the story is also picked up by both Karen and Margo. The multi-voiced narration highlights the fact that all of these parties have an individual investment in Eve's career rise. Their respective voices establish their ownership over the story. Narrating events from three different, and often contrary, points of view also builds a more complete picture of Eve.

It is worth asking why Mankiewicz has chosen these three characters to present the narrative. Their paths intersect with Eve's, but so, too, do Bill's, Lloyd's and Birdie's. Each of the three narrators focuses on the facts as they know them and the aspects of the story that specifically affect them. Each has a distinctive voice and the three differing angles provide an effective contrast, though none are completely objective. Their insights are inevitably limited by perspective, circumstance and bias. Moreover, the extent to which we identify with these individuals varies. It is easier, for example, to empathise with Karen than Addison. In the case of Margo, her role as one of the narrators enables the audience to connect more sympathetically with her, despite her flaws.

Addison's voice is dry and ironic, as befits his role as a theatre critic and commentator: a role that requires impartiality and professional detachment. However, Addison can be driven by spite and vested interest – his favourable review of Eve's first performance is calculated to demean Margo as much as to praise her young understudy – and his personal appraisal of Eve becomes coloured by the fact that she rejects his overtures.

By contrast, Karen's tone is more reflective and increasingly regretful. Of the three, Karen is the best placed to deliver a reliable narration as she is a fair-minded and forgiving woman whose measured restraint contrasts with Margo's volatility. But Karen's sense of betrayal is profound. She cannot possibly be objective towards the woman who exploits her friendship, blackmails her and tries to steal her husband. Margo's sense of grievance towards Eve is also strong. Her initial concern for Eve deteriorates into jealousy and, finally, sour hostility – all of which is reflected in her narration.

The title

Do we learn 'all about Eve'? The title suggests an exposé but, to a certain extent, Eve Harrington remains an elusive creation. With spurious modesty, Eve calls herself 'an apprentice in the theatre'. In fact, she is continually playing a part and the real woman behind the actress is concealed by layers of artifice and deception. Eve has invented a character in the same way that she does on stage and her self-assurance gives the role a compelling authenticity. It is arguable whether she herself can separate reality from the illusion.

Furthermore, Eve is only ever seen from the outside. What we do learn is presented entirely through the subjective filter of various characters' perspectives – all of whom become increasingly disillusioned with Eve's scheming. As has been noted, each of the three narrators has their own good reason for resenting Eve. The audience is ultimately presented with a negative version of Eve, built up from the combined views of those around her. Eve's own voice is silent. By the conclusion of the film, few concrete details have emerged and certainly no mitigating circumstances that might justify her behaviour. When Addison confronts her with her past, she has little to say. In this sense, Eve is unmasked rather than explained.

Reading film as text

All About Eve is a film and, as such, any analysis of it should use film language and refer to the particular qualities that characterise this form. While there are elements common to all narrative texts – such as characters, themes and values – there are also features specific to cinema. How do these elements combine to create meaning and reinforce the underlying concerns of the text?

Mise en scène

Mise en scène refers to the visual and design elements of a film. Everything we see in the frame – sets, locations, costumes and lighting – has been deliberately selected and is encoded with meaning. For instance, background details can provide ironic commentary on events taking place in the foreground (such as the foreshadowing offered by the 'Handle with Care' label backstage in Chapter 4). Another example is the close-up of the Sarah Siddons portrait at the conclusion of Bill's party. Mankiewicz implies here that Siddons is silently judging the antics of Margo and her guests, the picture acting as a silent reprimand towards those who aspire to emulate her example.

Actors and acting

The film features a brilliant ensemble cast and, in particular, showcases several great female performances. Bette Davis is unforgettable as theatrical diva Margo Channing and, as Margo, has some of the most memorable lines. Davis captures the extremes of the actress's mercurial personality, from cantankerous to vulnerable, in a way that ultimately elicits our sympathy. Anne Baxter is equally effective as the aspiring ingenue Eve Harrington, whose meek diffidence disguises self-serving menace.

The lead actors are ably supported by Celeste Holm as Karen Richards, Margo's best friend, who acts as a foil to Margo's excesses. George Sanders as the urbane theatre critic Addison DeWitt is another outstanding characterisation; his caustic elegance won Sanders the Oscar for Best Supporting Actor.

Costume

Costumes help define character. The wardrobe that Edith Head designed for Bette Davis as Margo conveys a strong, stylish personality who still wants to project sex appeal. At the same time, the fact that Margo is prepared to look 'like a junkyard' in front of her younger lover reflects both her confidence and the easy intimacy of the relationship.

Setting

Colour was readily available when *All About Eve* was made, but the monochromatic tones complement the drama being played out. Most of the film's scenes are shot indoors and many of the interiors, significantly, are set in the theatre, either backstage or on the stage itself. The central image of the theatrical setting reinforces the idea that this is a drama about people who create and labour in this space. It is also a reminder that the relationship between illusion and reality can be distorted. The few exterior scenes are still deliberately contained; for example, in Lloyd's stalled car, or outside the Shubert Theatre. This maintains the essential theatricality of the film.

Cinematography: framing and camera angles

Cinematically, *All About Eve* is conservative. The strength of the film lies in its sophisticated dialogue and characterisations, rather than striking visuals or innovative technical devices. The camerawork is straightforward and conventional, with the camera usually positioned at eye level in order to focus on the verbal exchanges between the characters. At times we could almost be watching a filmed play.

Nevertheless, in any scene, the placement of the camera is a key consideration. Shooting a character from above or below can alter our perception of the situation they are in and may suggest either empowerment or weakness. For example, the chairman of the Sarah Siddons Society is filmed with a low-angle shot when he is speaking, in order to emphasise his authority.

How a scene is framed – that is, the visual images on the screen and the way in which these are arranged – is also revealing. In *All About Eve*, Mankiewicz often positions his characters side by side or opposite each other as they interact. Again, there is a staged quality to this. The emphasis is on the relationships between the characters, the conflicts that emerge and the choices that they make.

Sound

Alfred Newman's original score consists of the main theme, featured in the opening and closing credits, and different musical leitmotifs (themes associated with particular characters) for Eve and each narrator. These range from the rather menacing theme that identifies Addison to the sweeter, more pensive melody that accompanies Karen's narration.

In addition to Newman's score, other music is used, reflecting the emotional state of particular characters or situations. For example, 'Liebestraum No. 3' (Franz Liszt) is played by pianist Claude Stroud at Bill's party, where a very drunk Margo insists on hearing it over and over again because it matches her self-indulgent mood. It is later heard again on the radio as Margo and Karen wait in the car, though here, Margo immediately turns it off, perversely declaring, 'I detest cheap sentiment'. Appropriately, 'Stormy Weather' is also heard in the background at Bill's party after Margo has insulted most of her guests.

Note: further film terminology may be found in 'Vocabulary for writing on *All About Eve*' (pp.69–70).

SCENE-BY-SCENE ANALYSIS

Chapter divisions used are those in the DVD of *All About Eve*.

Chapter 1: opening credits

A musical flourish, reminiscent of Twentieth Century Fox's signature fanfare – for which composer Alfred Newman is most famous – opens the film. This signals that *All About Eve* will be about theatre and the people who work in it. As the opening credits roll, the fanfare then merges into a bright, energetic version of the main theme. This is the leitmotif that is identified with Eve and her activities throughout.

Chapter 2

Summary: *At the annual dinner of the Sarah Siddons Society, acting's highest honour is about to be awarded to newcomer Eve Harrington.*

All About Eve begins with a close-up of the Sarah Siddons award, which takes pride of place on the award table. The award is a significant motif in the text, symbolising ambition and the pinnacle of achievement. It also represents the theatre itself as an institution of artistic integrity and continuity.

The occasion is introduced by Addison DeWitt's mocking voiceover. In a smug, self-serving tone, he presents his own credentials and then offers us a quick sketch of the main players in the drama about to unfold. This suggests that, despite the title, the film will be at least as much about the individuals who have shared Eve's story as about Eve herself. The medium close-ups of those characters intimately connected to the young actress also reveal that they do not share in the room's general enthusiasm. Lloyd Richards looks decidedly uncomfortable, Bill Sampson is scowling and Karen Richards appears detached, while Margo Channing needs a stiff drink in order to tolerate the ceremony.

The *mise en scène* of the Sarah Siddons Society's dining hall conveys a rather faded grandeur, as well as a strong sense of theatrical tradition. The room is crowded, hinting perhaps that the function has outgrown its premises. Pictures on the walls depict theatrical luminaries from the past who preside complacently over their acolytes (followers or devotees). A row of elderly waiters, coupled with Addison's comment that the windows in the dining room have not been opened since Mansfield's day (in the early 1900s), implies that some theatrical conventions are becoming stale and insular. Eve is the youngest recipient ever to be given the Siddons award and, therefore, presents a challenge to the norm.

When Eve is introduced, a medium long shot of the room shows the extent of the esteem in which she is held. Standing, she is shot from below to emphasise her professional triumph. However, the accolades heaped on her by the chairman elicit a cynical grin from Addison. As the camera follows his knowing glances towards Karen and Margo, their mutual response again undermines the idea that those who are 'privileged to know' Eve admire and respect her. This cross-cutting clearly suggests that the 'golden girl' is not all she seems.

Mankiewicz draws attention to the hands of his characters. Karen and Margo's refusal to clap distances them from the other guests, reinforcing their disapproval of Eve. Eve's own hands are grasping and, despite their grace in repose, their initial stillness belies her obsessive purpose. As she stretches out for the coveted award, the gesture epitomises the single-minded pursuit of her goals and the refusal to allow anything to get in her way. At exactly this moment, the camera pauses in a freeze-frame. The still of Eve is cross-cut to a close-up of Addison, whose narration continues.

Key vocabulary

Thespis: ancient Greek poet who is credited with being the first actor or 'thespian'.

Q Why does Mankiewicz elect to start the film at this point in the story?

Chapter 3

Summary: *Karen meets Eve.*

The camera moves in slowly to a close-up of Karen; her voiceover picks up the narrative and a flashback takes us back eight months. A dissolve connects the present and the past.

A long shot shows the theatre where Margo is performing *Aged in Wood* and, as befits her star status, her name is in lights above the title. The night is dark and 'drizzly' and Eve, significantly, emerges from the shadows into the harsher light of the alley. Her new identity is about to be revealed, but the persona is a covert one, mired in subterfuge and deception. Eve has done her homework. She knows, of course, that Karen is Margo Channing's best friend and can lead her to the celebrated actress.

Karen is dressed in a magnificent fur; she looks prosperous and therefore, despite her self-effacing disclaimer, a woman of potential influence. By contrast, Eve has chosen her plain trench coat and dowdy hat carefully in order to present herself as a respectable, but impecunious (penniless) young woman.

Chapter 4

Summary: *Karen takes Eve backstage to meet Margo in her dressing room with Lloyd and Birdie.*

The *mise en scène* backstage depicts organised chaos – the jumble of props and artefacts is the antithesis of the staged façade viewed by the audience. Eve's fascination is genuine. Karen watches sympathetically as the young woman is drawn straight to the stage, commenting on the atmosphere, 'You can breathe it, can't you – like some magic perfume'. The crate outside Margo's dressing room warns 'Handle with Care', signifying the destructive impact Eve will have in the lives of the people she is about to meet.

Margo, as in many subsequent scenes, is in front a mirror. Mirrors are used throughout the film as a symbol of society's obsession with self-image and the resistance to ageing. Paradoxically, like the theatre itself, mirrors can reflect the truth by presenting an illusion. In this scene, Margo, characteristically, is playing a part, acting out an interview she has just given. As she does so, the framing of the scene emphasises the affectionate intimacy of the Richardses, positioned between Margo and Birdie, with Karen on Lloyd's knee.

When Eve is introduced, she deftly strikes a balance between answering questions, eliciting information and flattering Margo. A close-up of her face, as she describes her devotion to Margo, expresses vulnerability and sincerity, but also flashes of the dangerous intensity that lies just beneath the surface.

Q What are your first impressions of these characters?

Chapter 5

Summary: *Eve tells her story to a sympathetic audience; Bill arrives to collect Margo, before leaving for the airport.*

As a wistful version of her theme music plays, Eve presents her story to Karen, Lloyd and Margo. The medium close-ups show the sympathy all three feel for the young war widow who dreams of working in the theatre. Again, Eve has done her homework and is able to incorporate personal details, like Lloyd's war record, into the conversation. The impression she conveys is of disarming innocence.

Eve's theme moves into the minor register as she relates Eddie's death. Eve's plucky, direct gaze contrasts with Margo's downcast expression, while Karen clasps Lloyd's arm for reassurance. By the time Eve has finished, she has manipulated her audience successfully – Margo is blowing her nose, and even Birdie retracts her comments. However, as Birdie rebuts the accusation that she was a 'fifth-rate vaudevillian', the frame includes Eve's reflection in Margo's mirror, literally watching over Margo's shoulder. This suggests that, from now on, Eve will be a constant and, ultimately, invasive presence in the actress's life.

Bill's entrance is timed against Birdie's exit, so that the doors closing and opening, after the stillness of Eve's monologue, bring some energy back into the room.

Q How is the relationship between the four friends – Margo, Bill, Karen and Lloyd – established?

Chapter 6

Summary: *Eve and Bill discuss his decision to work in Hollywood.*

Eve's unwavering gaze as she watches Bill snooze is both speculative and predatory. While she challenges his decision to go to Hollywood, there is also genuine curiosity in her expression. The low-angle shot of Bill while he expounds on the diverse possibilities offered by theatre emphasises his passion and credibility. When he is in the frame with Eve, he towers over her, which also confers authority.

As Margo re-emerges from the bathroom, she tells Birdie to look in her wig for a lost earring, prompting Bill's observation: 'Real diamonds in a wig – the world we live in!' The juxtaposition encapsulates the uneasy tension between reality and illusion that will be played out through the film.

Key vocabulary

Stanislavski: Russian theatre director, working around the early 1900s, and founder of the 'method' school of acting.

Chapter 7

Summary: *Margo and Eve farewell Bill at the airport; Eve goes home with Margo.*

When Bill calls Margo a 'loose lamb in a jungle', echoing Margo's (erroneous) view that Eve is 'a lamb loose in our big stone jungle', a clear connection is drawn between the two women.

The close-ups of Margo and Bill as they make their farewells emphasise their intimacy. Margo's insecurities are evident here – up until now, she has presented as self-assured and in complete control. Eve watches Margo closely and, after the couple have parted, she almost touches Margo's turned back in an ambiguous gesture that conveys a mixture of sympathy and desire. Ironically, the film cuts to Bill calling out, 'Keep your eye on her – don't let her get lonely'. Eve intends to do exactly that, and more.

As Margo's voiceover takes up the story, she slides her arm through Eve's, suggesting a growing warmth and friendship. Margo's theme music is heard in the background and carries over into the next scene.

Key point

Eve cleverly takes advantage of Margo and Bill's desire for privacy and makes herself as useful as possible. It is the start of her campaign to further her own acting ambitions by exploiting her relationship with Margo.

Q Discuss the lamb metaphor as it applies to these two women.

Q What dramatic ironies are evident in this scene?

Chapter 8

Summary: *Eve becomes Margo's new personal assistant, making herself indispensable both at home and at the theatre.*

Margo's voiceover gleefully relates the 'honeymoon' period with Eve: 'the next three weeks were out of a fairytale and I was Cinderella in the last act'. However, the wordless contest between Birdie and Eve to answer the telephone and the discord in the music hint at Birdie's resentment regarding the new arrangement. Her obvious umbrage, Eve's sunny efficiency and Margo's self-satisfaction present a contrast that hints at future conflict.

Mankiewicz uses a fade-out to connect this short scene with the next. The dissolve into black becomes the curtain rising on the cast of

Aged in Wood bowing to the audience. When Margo takes her applause, she is in the centre of the frame, brightly lit by the footlights and shot from underneath, every inch the star. This is cross-cut with close-ups of Eve watching from the shadowy wings; the expression on her face reveals an avid longing.

Later, when Eve holds up Margo's dress and bows to an imaginary audience, the gesture replicates Margo's own and highlights the extent of Eve's fantasies. At this point, though, Margo is flattered by the young woman's obvious hero-worship and her response to Eve is indulgent, even maternal. The fade-out concluding this scene marks a change in the dynamic between Margo and Eve.

Chapter 9

Summary: *Margo receives a phone call from Bill on his birthday; Birdie expresses her concerns.*

The phone call that Margo receives at three in the morning is one example too many of Eve's initiative. The close-up of Margo frowning when she finally works out who placed the call, coupled with her reaching for a cigarette, conveys her disquiet.

The fact that Margo is still smoking pensively the next morning suggests that she has continued to brood. Birdie's observations confirm her fears; Eve acts 'like an agent with only one client', dedicating excessive attention to her. Birdie notes shrewdly that Eve is modelling herself on Margo; Eve then arrives wearing Margo's hand-me-down suit, symbolising the way in which she is sartorially (relating to clothing) stepping into the character and appropriating Margo's identity. Eve's confidence in her role is such that she is oblivious to the undercurrents in the room and Margo's suppressed hostility. The knowing look that passes between Birdie and Margo after Eve has left expresses their mutual disapproval of the young woman, while the music – an ominous version of Eve's theme played in a minor key – foreshadows the breakdown of Margo and Eve's relationship.

Chapter 10

Summary: *Eve has organised a welcome-home and birthday party for Bill on his return from Hollywood; Margo picks a fight over Eve.*

Margo's voiceover again introduces the scene, gloomily announcing her sense of imminent disaster. Bill's welcome-home party is compared to 'the Chicago fire' (a massive fire in 1871 that destroyed much of the city) or 'the massacre of the Huguenots' (a French religious group persecuted in the seventeenth and eighteenth centuries). Margo has started drinking even before Birdie intimates the reason for Bill's tardiness. The rapport between them is such that Birdie can communicate her point (that Bill has been waylaid downstairs with Eve) with her body language alone. Margo feigns indifference, but her anxiety is clear when she runs across the landing and down the stairs.

Like Birdie, Bill reads Margo's mood immediately, but his refusal to be drawn into a defensive position reveals how even-handed this relationship is. Even as Margo whips herself 'up into a jealous froth', a part of her knows that she is overreacting. At the same time, as we will later learn, her instincts regarding Eve's motives are correct. Margo's rage and frustration are, somewhat comically, expressed by furiously popping a chocolate in her mouth, even though she feels she shouldn't. The argument is interrupted by Eve, its very source.

Chapter 11

Summary: *Karen, Lloyd and Max arrive; Eve is introduced to Addison DeWitt; Margo gets very drunk; she asks Max to find Eve a job in his office.*

Lloyd's description of the 'Macbeth-ish' atmosphere pinpoints the uncomfortable sense of menace in the room (in spite of the bright, jolly piano music): 'What has, or is about to happen?' As the camera looks up at Margo, emphasising her control, she responds after a dramatic pause by instructing her friends to fasten their seatbelts, in preparation for the 'bumpy night'.

Addison DeWitt's arrival at the party, accompanied by Claudia Casswell, brings him back into the drama. When Eve is introduced to

Addison, the framing of the scene emphasises the significance of this meeting. We view them in profile as they face each other, each calculating the possible benefits that might be forthcoming. Their encounter is offset by the unlikely chorus of Margo and Claudia standing between them; Margo's jaded sarcasm is punctuated by Claudia's naive frivolity.

By the time Margo has downed an ill-advised number of martinis, her mood has deteriorated from punchy to despondent. As she confesses her self-doubts to Lloyd, 'Blue Moon' (Rodgers and Hart) is played in the background, reflecting her emotional state.

Q Discuss Margo's response to turning forty: 'Now I suddenly feel as if I've taken all my clothes off'. Does it show weakness or pragmatism?

Chapter 12

Summary: *Eve asks Karen to help her get Margo's understudy role; Addison and Bill discuss the theatre.*

Fur coats are a ubiquitous image in the film and an obvious, visible sign of success. Karen and Margo are regularly draped in furs to protect against the icy New York winter. By contrast, in Hollywood, 'it never even gets cold', but that does not stop the visiting Hollywood movie star from flaunting a magnificent sable. As well as symbolising the wealth and ostentation of the world that she comes from, the sable encapsulates Hollywood's allure. Claudia says covetously, 'Now there's something a girl could make sacrifices for' and, according to Bill, she 'probably has'.

Mankiewicz's framing of a scene on the staircase is interesting; his characters sit casually on the stairs, ranked in tiers. This enables them to engage in an illuminating discussion on the theatre business, while the image figuratively evokes the idea of a hierarchical profession. Claudia, as befits her neophyte (beginner) status, is on the bottom rung. Eve, a few steps above Claudia, rejects Bill's claim that the theatre offers little reward for the extreme sacrifice involved. She betrays her own craving for affirmation – 'Why, if there's nothing else, there's applause' – and Addison's raised eyebrow indicates his surprise at her disclosure. He will use this knowledge of Eve's ambition to promote his own ends.

Chapter 13

Summary: *Margo is rude to her guests.*

By this stage, Margo is ready to quarrel with everyone over nothing. Karen resents her rudeness and stands up to her: 'Stop being a star and stop treating your guests as your supporting cast'. In fact, all those who care about Margo – Karen, Lloyd, Bill and Birdie – stand up to her at different times and confront her with some home truths. By contrast, Eve never does. Addison observes the altercation with his customary detachment, commenting cynically as Bill follows Margo upstairs: 'Too bad, we're going to miss the third act'.

Despite Eve's apparent distress at incurring Margo's displeasure, her last thought is to remind the unsuspecting Karen of her promise. The medium close-up of Eve shows her calculating mind, revealing her real priority.

Featuring prominently in this scene is the Sarah Siddons portrait that hangs beside Margo's staircase. At one point, while Margo and the Richardses argue, the actress's image peers regally over their shoulders. The scene concludes with a close-up of the picture which acts as a judgement on the foibles and weaknesses of those working in the theatre. It is also a timely reminder that fame brings unexpected costs.

Key point

The 'night to go down in history' is the turning point in Margo's relationship with Eve. Margo's goodwill has been eroded and she now views Eve as a threat. Henceforth, Eve will pursue her own agenda more blatantly.

Chapter 14

Summary: *Margo arrives late for Claudia Casswell's audition and discovers from Addison that Eve has read, brilliantly, in her place.*

As Margo's theme music is heard, a long shot shows her getting out of a taxi in front of the theatre. Dashing inside, she passes the promotional poster that features an unmistakable drawing of her *Aged in Wood* character. A smaller version of this also hangs in her dressing room. Both reinforce her iconic status in the theatre.

This is about to be challenged by the upstart Eve's performance. Addison raves about Eve's reading, presenting it as the kind of rare moment for which 'all true believers' such as himself 'wait and pray'. He clearly enjoys twisting the knife (even though he says Margo herself was once such a moment too) as he describes the effect of the reading on those present – Lloyd, in particular, was 'beside himself'. At this point, Addison has no vested interest in Eve's career, but his eulogistic response does confirm her ability. Margo's fury is such that she does not even acknowledge the hapless Miss Casswell, emerging from the ladies' room.

Chapter 15

Summary: *Margo fights with Max, Lloyd and, finally, Bill.*

In the theatre, Max is warned of the imminent confrontation when, instead of responding to his greeting, Margo swings her fur over his head in contempt. As Margo sarcastically accuses Max of being devious, a close-up emphasises her controlled rage. Eve knows that the best strategy is to back off quietly and let the men fight her battles.

Throughout the subsequent shouting match with Lloyd and Max, Margo is filmed from an audience perspective, looking up at her on the stage. This reminds us that she is, as Addison described in Chapter 2, 'a star of the theatre ... a great star, a true star. She never was, or will be, anything less or anything else'. The camera angle also increases her authority, which goes beyond merely having the upper hand as the star of the show; it has a moral value. Margo's accusations against Eve may seem grossly unfair to those around her, but, in fact, her 'feeling' that Eve is plotting against her is the truth. Margo tries, and fails, to put this into words with Bill: 'Not nonsense'. Unfortunately, having afforded him too much cause in the past to mistrust her 'paranoiac tantrums', he cannot give her the benefit of the doubt in this case. The heated exchange between them is shot in a series of close-ups, highlighting the crisis in their relationship. The final high overhead shot shows Margo alone and vulnerable on the stage bed – the location emphasising the links between the theatre and her personal life (represented by the domestic image of the bed).

Q Comment on Margo's 'childish little game of cat and mouse'. Why does she address the issue in this way?

Q Discuss the implications of Bill's statement, 'You know there isn't a playwright in the world who could make me believe this would happen between two adult people'.

Chapter 16

Summary: *After hearing of the afternoon's events, Karen decides to teach Margo a lesson; the Richardses and Margo go out of town for the weekend and, on the way back, the car runs out of fuel; Lloyd goes in search of assistance; and Karen and Margo talk frankly as they wait.*

Lloyd's effusive enthusiasm for Eve's talent is undercut by Karen's dry response, 'Don't run out of adjectives, dear'. The Richardses are usually filmed in the frame together, even when they are arguing, which emphasises their closeness as a couple. Here, they are in complete agreement with regard to Margo's bad behaviour.

As Karen's theme music is heard in the background, her voiceover explains how she arrived at her 'big idea'. She rationalises that 'the boot would land where it would do the most good for all concerned'. However, despite Karen's worthy intentions, her 'perfectly harmless joke' is predicated on Eve's discretion and goodwill, neither of which will be forthcoming.

As Karen's narration continues, a long shot establishes the country context, showing the Richardses' car driving through a dark, snowy landscape. Margo's humorous comment about their underwear begins to dispel the tension, but immediately the car runs out of fuel, and Karen's close-up gives away the fact that she is the one responsible.

What follow is a pivotal, candid conversation between the two women as they wait in the car, with Margo sharing her emotional needs and anxieties with her closest friend. The scene is filmed at close range, the camera reinforcing Karen and Margo's mutual intimacy by concentrating on their faces. There is also dramatic irony: at the very time when Margo is berating herself for treating Eve 'pretty disgracefully', the latter is making the most of her opportunity to upstage her 'idol' in *Aged in Wood*. Furthermore, although neither Margo nor Karen realise it yet, describing Eve as 'so feminine and so helpless' is equally incongruous. Finally, after Karen's teary apology, Margo philosophically dismisses it as 'one of destiny's merry pranks', reasoning that 'after all, you didn't personally drain the gasoline tank yourself'.

Chapter 17

Summary: *On his way to congratulate Eve, Addison overhears her propositioning Bill, then offers his support when Bill rebuffs her.*

Addison's rather discordant motif is played as he goes backstage. Like Eve, he comes from the shadows and, initially, is shot from behind. The tone of his voiceover indicates that he is more than aware of Eve's motives regarding her 'thoughtful' invitation to attend the theatre that afternoon and the 'happy coincidence' that so many reviewers witnessed her performance.

After Bill's rejection, Eve's response illustrates her volatility and invites the audience's mistrust. Firstly, she shows her rage by throwing an ugly tantrum and pulling her wig apart. Then, at Addison's knock, she switches instantly from fury to charm. The whole performance is unexpected and disturbing.

Addison's interest is edifying and soothes Eve's bruised ego. As the two converse, a number of close-ups suggest a shared understanding. However, Addison sees through her false modesty and requests 'a minimum of pretending' between them.

Key point

Eve's dubious alliance with Addison DeWitt is cemented in this scene. The relationship involves a clear choice that will polarise her from her former friends. In addition, by putting herself in his hands, Eve inadvertently gives him licence to control her career.

Key vocabulary

Svengali: a fictional character capable of controlling those around him through hypnosis.

Chapter 18

Summary: *Karen reads Addison's review of Eve's performance; Bill and Margo are reconciled.*

The fact that Addison and Eve are lunching at '21' with a movie talent scout shows that events are moving quickly for the young actress. Addison's blanket assumption that she has 'no intention of going to Hollywood' is refuted by Eve's expression, implying that there are already differences brewing between the two.

Idly reading Addison's review as she waits for Margo, Karen's response is communicated through her body language. The audience does not see her face, but her distress is clear when her hand reaches blindly for the arm of the chair.

Addison's vitriolic editorial comments about the 'lamentable practice' of ageing actresses monopolising roles for which they are clearly too old strike Margo where she is most exposed. The lamb metaphor turns sour when she threatens to 'stuff that pathetic little lost lamb down Mr DeWitt's ugly throat'. When Bill arrives, she is happy to be looked after.

Chapter 19

Summary: *Karen and Lloyd discuss Addison's review, disagreeing on Eve's motives and whether or not she should play the part of Cora.*

Lloyd asserts that Addison is the villain and Eve an 'impulsive kid' who has had her words twisted by a 'professional manure slinger', while Karen calls Eve 'a contemptible little worm', leaving no doubt as to where her sympathies now lie. Karen argues that Eve's gall is such that she would ask 'Abbot to give her Costello'. The scene demonstrates Lloyd's gullibility and how easily he is manipulated by seemingly vulnerable women. Conversely, the extent to which he relies on his wife is also evident. Ironically, when Karen asks that he refer 'all of Miss Eve Harrington's future requests to me', she does not anticipate that she will, in fact, be blackmailed by Eve over the contentious role.

Key vocabulary

Abbot and Costello: famous American comedy duo of the 1940s and 1950s.

Q Does this scene reinforce gender stereotypes? If so, how?

Chapter 20

Summary: *Karen and Lloyd dine with Margo and Bill who announce their engagement; Addison and Eve are also together at the Cub Room.*

Margo's adoring looks towards Bill as he praises her performance reveal her happiness and the audience is reminded of Karen's comment, 'They'd die without each other'. The four friends affirm their friendship and share their pleasure at the impending nuptials: 'The world is full of love tonight'. They are so caught up with each other that they do not notice Addison and Eve until Karen receives Eve's note, asking to see her in the ladies' room.

The camera chronicles their collective disapproval of 'Rasputin' (Addison), who cuts a lonely figure at the opposite table. Karen snubs him as she sails past to discover what is going on in Eve's 'feverish little brain'. Margo and Bill display their scorn for Addison by parodying his toast with their celery.

Key vocabulary

Rasputin: controversial adviser and confidant to the last Russian Tsarina Alexandra Romanov.

Chapter 21

Summary: *Eve blackmails Karen over the part of Cora.*

The close-ups between Karen and Eve as the latter 'explains' herself chart the shifting power play between the two women. At first, Karen is resistant and disbelieving. The turning point is when Eve starts to cry; Karen is too kind-hearted not to modify her tone. Eve successfully manoeuvres the whole conversation so that, in the end, her demand for the role of Cora has a kind of brazen inevitability. Her gloating expression dispels any further doubt as to her motives. In contrast, the mid-shot of Karen, left alone in the ladies' room, conveys her bewilderment and distress.

With supreme confidence, Eve unwisely attempts to manipulate Addison in the same way she has used the others. She erroneously misreads his motives and, therefore, overestimates her ability to 'manage' him. This is foreshadowed when she tells Addison that she 'needs' him, which invites the potentially sinister assurance: 'I intend to hold you to it'.

Q How 'clever' is Eve?

Chapter 22

Summary: *Karen rejoins her friends; Margo announces she does not want the role of Cora.*

The emotional divide between Karen and Margo is symbolised by the framing. Mankiewicz shows the two couples in separate pairs as they converse. At this point, despite their intimacy, they are not all on the same wavelength: Karen is preoccupied and nervous and Lloyd tentatively defends Eve, while Bill and Margo are so euphoric that they notice little else. Margo's joy means that she can even be magnanimous towards Eve.

Although seated side by side, Karen and Margo are not filmed together in the same frame until Margo announces that she no longer wants to play Cora. This underscores the fact that the crisis has now passed and the friendship is no longer under threat. By the end of the scene, all four friends are again shot in the frame together.

Chapter 23

Summary: *Rehearsals for* Footsteps on the Ceiling *commence, with Eve playing Cora; Eve manipulates Lloyd; Addison goes to New Haven for the opening.*

The few seconds of darkness that precede this scene hint at the discord that is about to unfold. Karen's pensive voiceover tells of the friction during rehearsals for the new play. Feeling increasingly marginalised, she watches silently from the stalls as relationships unravel. The shot of her leaving the theatre depicts her very much as an outsider.

The next scene is still presented from Karen's point of view. A high overhead shot of her in bed, ruminating over Eve's adverse presence in their lives, emphasises her sense of helplessness. The telephone call from the young woman who says she 'room[s] across the hall' from Eve then exemplifies Eve's controlling influence. While Eve and her friend congratulate themselves on the success of their ruse, Lloyd's guilt and Karen's apprehension suggest a marriage under strain. This downturn of events, from Karen's perspective, is reflected in the melancholy soundtrack.

By contrast, Addison and Eve present a united and convivial front in New Haven, strolling to the hotel. At this point, they are filmed in the frame together: 'killer to killer'. Both are confident that it will be 'a night to remember'.

Q Why does Karen decide to 'skip rehearsals'?

Q Discuss Karen's statement: 'It seemed to me that I had always known that it would happen. And here it was.' What is Karen thinking of here?

Chapter 24

Summary: *Eve tells Addison that she plans to marry Lloyd Richards; Addison blackmails Eve into compliance.*

The positioning of the camera in this scene signifies shifts in the power balance. At first, Addison, still seated, is caught unawares by Eve's disclosure that she and Lloyd intend to marry. The camera looks down on Addison and up at Eve, who feels very much in control of her future. She even denies consummating the relationship with Lloyd, arguing she wants a 'run-of-the-play contract' – the suggestion being that she will not allow any messy romantic entanglements to interfere with her career plans.

However, the dynamic alters when Addison rises to his feet. Throughout the confrontation, he is filmed from below to emphasise his dominance. After unpacking her lies one by one, he asks contemptuously if she still insists that Lloyd is in love with her. By this stage, Eve has been completely discredited. A mournful cello underscores her wretchedness as a high-angle shot shows her lying on the bed. Addison's scornful prediction – 'You'll give the performance of your life' – links this scene to the next.

Q What do we learn about Addison DeWitt from this scene? Why does he want Eve?

Chapter 25

Summary: *Eve accepts her award, but does not attend the after-party in her honour.*

The narrative returns to Addison's voiceover accompanying the still of Eve accepting the Siddons award. Eve continues to give a flawless performance as the gracious young recipient of the theatre's highest prize. Addressing her audience with measured poise, she is dressed in a glittering gown and filmed with a low-angle shot.

Addison watches with customary scorn, his trademark cigarette-holder in hand. When Eve tells her audience that 'everything wise and witty has long since been said', her words have a mocking resonance in light of the punishment she must accept at Addison's hands. As Eve gives individual praise to all those who have helped her, the cross-cutting between medium close-ups of each attests to their antagonism and emphasises the moral divide between them.

Eve affirms that 'the theatre ... has given me all I have'. However, the text has argued that those who are driven by false values, such as greed and dishonesty, gain little of worth. Eve's material reward is small compensation for her spiritual impoverishment.

Key point

Margo, Bill, Karen and Lloyd have all had their security and complacency challenged by Eve's intervention in their lives. The insight that they take away from events results in a subtle shift in how they view the world and each other. The film demonstrates that those characters with a 'heart' have the capacity to learn from experience. Conversely, those with 'no heart to burn' (as Bill says of Addison in Chapter 11) essentially remain the same.

Chapter 26

Summary: *Eve returns to her apartment; she is surprised by a young intruder.*

Eve does not even say goodnight to Addison after his cab drops her off. She can win the small victories with him, such as refusing to attend the party, but not the larger ones, and her resentment is clear. The *mise en scène* in Eve's bedroom corroborates her intention to stay in Hollywood for as long as she can. Half-packed trunks and suitcases fill the room. The strain of the evening shows when Eve immediately gets herself a drink, refuting her previous assertion that 'I never have any' (Chapter 24). It is also the only time the audience sees her smoke – this confirms the fact that Eve behaves very differently when her guard is down.

Eve's immediate suspicion of the intruder dissipates. Ironically, she is so egocentric that she fails to recognise in Phoebe the same hungry intensity that fuelled her own success. Phoebe, imagining herself emulating Eve's achievements, replicates Eve's earlier covert action of bowing to a fantasy audience while clutching Margo's gown. Mankiewicz also revisits the motif of hands. When Phoebe holds up Eve's evening coat to admire the image in the mirror, her hands covetously stroke the fabric. The gesture signifies a lust for stardom.

As Phoebe bows to the mirror, imagining the applause, she is surrounded by multiple reflections of herself. The image highlights the fact that neither Phoebe nor Eve is unique – there are thousands of girls with the same hopes and aspirations. The lure of stardom is so dazzling that it becomes all-consuming and obscures any other vision. Literally, all that these women see is themselves.

Q Comment on Mankiewicz's decision to introduce a new character in the final scene. How effective is this ending?

CHARACTERS & RELATIONSHIPS

Eve Harrington (Anne Baxter)

Key quotes

'No brighter light has ever dazzled the eye than Eve Harrington.' (Addison)

'Princess fire and music.' (Margo)

'Imagine: to know every night that different hundreds of people love you ... They want you. You belong. Just that alone is worth anything!'

'Eve Harrington' is, of course, a carefully crafted construct. Eve deliberately misrepresents herself from the beginning. Her real name is Gertrude Slescynski, a far less marketable moniker. Having turned her back on her past – her parents haven't heard from her in three years – she has manufactured a personal history, complete with the poignant loss of a young husband, and reinvented herself with the express purpose of furthering her own single-minded ambition.

The duplicitous way in which Eve behaves towards her 'friends' reveals an utterly unscrupulous young woman for whom lying is second nature. Like all proficient liars, she uses elements of the truth to enhance the effectiveness of her lies. She *does* admire Margo Channing, and *is* genuinely in love with the theatre – or at least the idea of being centre stage – and she *has* grown up in poverty. Furthermore, in order to give the part of 'Eve Harrington' complete integrity, perhaps she has to believe in her own fabrication. Ironically, Bill comments on Eve's 'lack of pretence' and, initially, what comes across is her apparent sincerity and desire to please.

Eve is always putting on a performance and playing to an audience. She is clearly a talented young actress and the unassuming front she presents to the world is utterly convincing. Even the cynical Birdie is moved when Eve tells her story in Margo's dressing room. Eve explains to this, her first audience, how 'acting and make-believe' filled her girlhood: 'It got so I couldn't tell the real from the unreal – except that the unreal seemed more real to me'. The lines between fantasy and reality are blurred and Eve's ability to separate the two is questionable.

Eve's youth may partially explain her tenacious drive to succeed, but her compete lack of conscience suggests a cold and manipulative personality. Eve sees people solely in terms of what they can offer her. She targets Karen Richards because the latter can introduce her to Margo Channing and Karen unsuspectingly – and ironically – likens Eve's devotion to Margo to 'something out of a book'. It is, in fact, a fiction, designed to facilitate the younger woman's obsessive climb to stardom.

Eve's ambition is toxic. She inveigles her way into Margo's household and affections with ease: 'Eve became my sister, lawyer, mother, friend, psychiatrist and cop'. However, after the 'honeymoon' period, Eve's strategy becomes clear, as does the threat she poses to Margo's career. Margo Channing has the life that Eve wants; she literally aspires to 'play' Margo. As Birdie notes, Eve is 'studying' the actress, as if she 'was a play or a book or a set of blueprints – how you walk, talk, eat, think, sleep'. Eve borrows Margo's mannerisms, wears her clothes and learns her lines. Becoming Margo's 'understudy' in the theatre echoes a process already well underway outside the theatre.

Eve's passion for the theatre is linked to her desire for personal affirmation and a sense of belonging. She equates the applause of an audience with love and has convinced herself that this is more important than anything else. When Eve bows to a fantasy audience as she holds up Margo's costume, she is imagining the 'waves of love coming over the footlights and wrapping' her up. By contrast, after a lifetime in front of audiences, Margo understands that their fickle approval is no substitute for real love.

Eve shows no loyalty to those who have helped and encouraged her but, with Machiavellian arrogance, focuses on her own agenda. She is prepared to blackmail Karen in order to get the part of Cora, saying she would 'do much more for a part that good'. Having abused Karen and Margo's trust, she subsequently tries to sabotage their personal relationships. After Eve has destroyed the collective goodwill, Margo christens her 'Little Miss Evil' (Chapter 22).

Eve tells Karen, 'I've always considered myself a very clever girl – smart, good head on my shoulders'. This is partially true but, like all narcissists, Eve's vision is clouded and she fails to appreciate the threat posed by Addison DeWitt when she encourages him to 'take charge'. While Eve is obviously sorry that Addison has caught her out, there is no evidence of remorse on her part or any suggestion that she has learned a lesson. Presumably, her hope in relocating to Hollywood is to escape Addison's sphere of influence. There is a hint of vulnerability at the end in Eve's loneliness and alienation, but the audience is positioned to feel that she has received exactly what she deserves. The clear implication is that Phoebe will show the same ruthlessness as Eve herself, and the narrative has come full circle.

Key point

Eve's journey to success comes at considerable personal cost. Her lack of empathy blindsides her to the consequences of her choices, but ultimately she discovers the folly of building a career based on lies and manipulation.

Margo Channing (Bette Davis)

Key quotes

'Ms Channing is ageless.'

'We know you … is it over, or is it just beginning?' (Karen)

'You're maudlin and full of self-pity. You're magnificent.' (Addison)

Margo Channing has been a star ever since her debut as a naked fairy in *A Midsummer Night's Dream* at the age of four. She is brilliant, gifted and formidable – a grand diva of the theatre. Margo is the quintessential professional and never misses a performance. As Karen explains, it is not so much a case of 'the show must go on', but of 'Margo must go on': 'if she can walk, crawl or roll, she plays'. Margo can be imperious, peremptory or acerbic, depending on her mood. Conversely, with close friends, she demonstrates a boisterous, even self-deprecating sense of humour and, in spite of her worldly cynicism, she can also be sentimental and soft-hearted. Margo is easily seduced by Eve's narrative of loss and hardship, and the close-up of her face as Eve tells her story is one of the earliest hints of the actress's soft centre.

From the opening scene, Margo is set up in opposition to Eve. She is, according to Addison, who is circumspect in his praise, a 'true star'. His tone implies that, as an actor, Margo has an integrity and charisma that is difficult to duplicate. Outwardly, the two women appear to have much in common. Both have rare talent and both will share stellar careers: Addison tells Margo that 'In time, she'll be what you are'. Furthermore, in claiming Margo as her 'benefactress and champion', Eve is cleverly positioning herself, by association, as Margo's natural successor. However, unlike Eve, Margo has not been prepared to sacrifice her essential humanity in the pursuit of fame. Eve (ironically) lauds her as the genuine article: 'a great actress and a great woman'.

Margo is often difficult and is famous for her histrionics; Lloyd contends that she has a genius for creating 'bar-room brawls' out of 'innocent misunderstandings'. In a frank moment, Margo confesses ruefully that 'infants behave the way I do', perhaps reflecting on her rudeness and maudlin self-pity during Bill's party. Despite the fact that she is often driven by her passions, Margo is no fool and she is one of the first to mistrust Eve's motives. The alarm bells go off after Eve places a birthday call to Bill on Margo's behalf and she starts to feel manipulated by the younger woman.

Insecurities

On face value, Margo has everything a woman could want. By general consensus, she is considered 'a great actress at the peak of her career' and enjoys all the material trappings that come with fame and success. Furthermore, she is in a committed relationship with a man who adores her and has a circle of loyal and loving friends. Yet, happiness eludes her. Margo has just turned forty and is ambivalent about the milestone: 'I hadn't quite made up my mind to admit it'. Like many actors, she is insecure and needs constant reassurance about her talent and desirability. She is more than conscious of ageing in a profession that places a premium on youth and beauty. Furthermore, Margo's insecurity is compounded by the fact that her lover, Bill Sampson, is eight years younger, and she is painfully aware of this age difference.

Margo is frightened of being alone, but wants to be loved for herself, as opposed to the glittering public image. In fact, she queries what 'Margo Channing' means at all – aside from a name in lights and a 'temperament'. She is hesitant to commit to the relationship with Bill, not because she doesn't love him, but because she worries that he is unable to separate the real woman from the actress. She is anxious that 'if I can't tell them apart, how can he?' Margo's monologue in the car with Karen is very revealing. Her envy of Eve's youth, femininity and apparent helplessness is driven by the cultural definition of what is considered attractive in a woman. Consequently, she admits that she wants to be all of these things for Bill. Margo sees 'being a woman' as a 'career' and insists to Karen that 'sooner or later, we've got to work at it, no matter how many other careers we've had or wanted'. She believes that without love 'you're not a woman' and favourable press clippings are a poor substitute for the lack of a fulfilling relationship. Even in this moment of candid self-reflection, Margo is the consummate actress, conscious of her audience: 'Slow curtain. The end'.

Key point

At the beginning of the film, Margo is at a professional and emotional crossroads. Her twin fears of ageing and losing Bill weigh heavily on her mind. However, 'the good that Eve leaves behind' invites a new perspective. Margo learns to trust and to prioritise, and gains a fresh confidence with regard to her professional options.

Karen Richards (Celeste Holm)

Key quotes

'... just a playwright's wife – I'm the lowest form of celebrity.'
'Happy little housewife.' (Margo)

Addison observes that Karen is of the theatre 'by marriage' (to Lloyd). She is 'fanatically devoted' to her husband and fiercely defensive of his talent and reputation. Ordinarily, she attends the rehearsals of his new plays, as well as off-Broadway openings – her absence from the rehearsals and the New Haven premiere of *Footsteps on the Ceiling* is pointed. In turn, Lloyd trusts his wife's judgement and relies on her advice. Before being diverted by Eve, he reassures Karen that he will not be making any changes to the casting of his new play without her input.

Karen's sympathetic kindness and trusting nature are evident from the outset. Karen accepts Eve's story on face value and spontaneously offers her friendship to the young woman after their first meeting. Lloyd later refers to Karen's 'bitter cynicism', but, in fact, she gives Eve the benefit of the doubt for as long as she is able. However, Eve's behaviour shows Karen that the world is not as well-intentioned as she had assumed.

Karen and Margo

Karen's upbringing has been very different from Margo's – when the latter is drunk, she disparagingly alludes to Karen's family wealth. Karen values the long friendship she has shared with Margo and her gracious dignity provides an effective balance to the actress's temperament. Generally, Karen makes allowances for Margo's tantrums, but she finds it difficult to tolerate bad manners or deliberate cruelty: 'It's about time Margo realised that what's attractive on stage need not necessarily be attractive off'. Karen's 'boot in the rear' to her close friend is well-meaning, though ill-advised, as it places Margo in Eve's power. When the prank backfires, Karen is horrified to find herself blackmailed by her erstwhile protégé.

Karen and Lloyd

Karen is rendered vulnerable by Eve's designs on her husband. Miserably, Karen senses Lloyd gravitating towards Eve and feels powerless: 'That helplessness you feel when you have no talent to offer, outside of loving your husband'. Eve's youth is presented as a threat to both Margo and Karen. Faced with a gifted and considerably more ruthless adversary, Karen despairs of competing: 'Everything Lloyd loved about me, he'd gotten used to long ago'. However, the pairing that Addison calls 'an unholy alliance' does not eventuate. At the Siddons banquet, Karen has Lloyd back by her side and has recovered her graceful composure, although she has too much pride to endorse Eve's success beyond a terse greeting at the close of the ceremony.

Addison DeWitt (George Sanders)

Key quotes

'I have lived in the theatre as a Trappist monk lives in his faith. I have no other world, no other life.'

'I'm nobody's fool – least of all yours.' (to Eve)

Addison's narration bookends the extended flashback that tells Eve's story. He introduces himself, with supreme arrogance, to those uninformed few who 'do not read, attend the theatre, listen to unsponsored radio programs or know anything of the world in which you live', explaining that he is 'essential' to the theatre, his 'natural habitat', though he admits that 'in it I toil not, neither do I spin'. His paraphrasing of Jesus' words from the Sermon on the Mount – referenced in the gospels of both Matthew and Luke – is revealing. Addison is implying that, like the lilies of the field and despite his apparent idleness, he rivals King Solomon 'in all his glory'. It is also a reference to Addison's status in the theatrical world. As a New York critic and commentator, he is immensely powerful, and young hopefuls, like Eve, read his daily column as if it were the Bible.

Addison's image

Addison's urbane image disguises an underlying hostility towards the world that feeds into, and poisons, his relationships. By his own admission, he is incapable of affection or loyalty. The vindictiveness that he can display in his reviews and his contemptuous, superior manner alienate many; therefore he is generally disliked, and certainly mistrusted, by the theatrical fraternity. Lloyd labels Addison a 'venomous fishwife'; to Margo, he is simply 'Rasputin'.

Of necessity, Addison is tolerated as an unavoidable evil. When he turns up, apparently uninvited, to Margo's party, Margo and her friends are cordial but aloof. Addison's young companion, Miss Casswell, is one of his projects. Addison sees himself as a patron of the arts and a nurturer of fresh talent – but only if there is something in it for him. Addison's sexuality is ambiguous, and although he clearly has relationships with women these are superficial at best and exploitative at worst.

Addison and Eve

Addison quickly recognises Eve's potential – he calls her reading 'a revelation' – and, correctly, senses a kindred spirit. He has a strong perception of his own 'otherness', telling Eve that they are both 'improbable' people who share a 'contempt for humanity, an inability to love and be loved, insatiable ambition and talent'. Addison's vanity is such that he assumes Eve will be flattered by his attentions, as so many others have been; he concludes that 'we deserve each other'. However, he miscalculates Eve's response and reacts violently to her scorn, for once letting his controlled mask slip: 'Now remember, as long as you live, never to laugh at me. At anything or anyone else, but never at me!' In demanding Eve's submission, Addison plainly enjoys the power he wields over her.

Bill Sampson (Gary Merrill)

Key quotes

'What I go after, I want to go after. I don't want it to come after me.'

'I'll marry you if it turns out you have no blood at all.' (Margo)

Bill is self-assured and confident, a young director whose star is in the ascent. Eve calls him 'the best and most successful young director in the theatre'. Bill's flourishing career on Broadway has not led to any misplaced snobbery with regard to directing in Hollywood and he is prepared to juggle both film and stage-work. In spite of Eve's observation that 'so few come back', he does return to the Broadway stage. Bill's views on the theatre are pragmatic and down-to-earth. He admits to Addison that the theatre contains a 'screwball element', but is adamant that the theatre could not survive unless it was predominantly about expertise and unadulterated hard work.

Similarly, Bill refuses to indulge the Margo Channing mystique; in his first scene, he tells her affectionately that she is 'looking like a junkyard!' He is sometimes tolerant of Margo's moods and is more inclined to disengage than be drawn in when she is throwing a tantrum. Bill admits to her that there are 'certain characteristics for which you are famous, on stage and off. I love you for some of them and in spite of others'. He recognises that these qualities are part of Margo's armoury and acknowledges that, in the theatrical 'rat-race', she has to 'keep her teeth sharp'. However, Bill insists, 'I will not have you sharpen them on me'. He has no hesitation in standing up to the star when he considers that she is being unreasonable, and he is a strong enough character to challenge her – even walk away from her – if necessary.

Despite Margo's concerns, Bill does love Margo for herself. He attempts to diffuse her fears regarding the age difference between them, dismissing her 'age obsession' as irrelevant paranoia. He rejects Eve's clumsy attempt at seduction and when Margo is humiliated by Addison's poisonous review, Bill immediately rushes to comfort her. In turn, Margo knows, even though he is 'conceited and thoughtless and messy', that they are lucky to have found each other.

Lloyd Richards (Hugh Marlowe)

Key quotes

'All playwrights should be dead for three hundred years.' (Margo)

'Lloyd Richards is commercially the most successful playwright in America ... and artistically, the most promising.' (Addison)

Lloyd is a contented man. He enjoys a happy marriage and is highly regarded in his profession. His plays have been effective vehicles for Margo Channing and both have done well from the partnership. Given that Lloyd is a writer, it is not surprising that he has some of the most articulate lines in the film. He can be eloquent – such as in his generous toast to Margo and Bill – or cutting, as the situation demands. In his heated exchange with Margo, the metaphors fly back and forth, with Lloyd, rather pompously, having the last word: 'It's about time the piano realised it has not written the concerto'.

Eve's entry into the Richardses' lives shatters Lloyd's complacency. Despite working in a cut-throat business like the theatre, he is curiously impressionable and is quite taken in by Eve's 'quality of quiet graciousness'. He continues to defend her, long after Karen and the others have recognised her blatant opportunism. By the time Addison's review is published, Lloyd still views Eve as a victim rather than a villain. Presumably, after summarily failing with Bill, Eve does try to seduce the more susceptible Lloyd, but to what extent she succeeds is left to the imagination of the audience. Certainly Addison dismisses her story of a proposed marriage as pure fantasy. The final affectionate exchange between Lloyd and Karen after the Siddons dinner, when he offers her his award, makes it clear that Lloyd's love and loyalty remain with his wife: 'For services rendered beyond the ... whatever-it-is of duty, darling'.

Max Fabian (Gregory Ratoff)

Key quotes

'Let the rest of the world beat their brains out for a buck.'

'Who am I to threaten? I'm a dying man.'

In accepting her award, Eve commends 'dear, sentimental, generous, courageous Max Fabian'. Unlike the others at his table, Max seems genuinely pleased at Eve's achievement. Or, perhaps, he is simply delighted that his gamble has paid off and his backers can recoup their investment. Addison indicates that Max is less interested in art for its own sake than in the profit margin of any given production. He has become a very successful Broadway producer by following his hunches. The fact that Max takes a chance on an 'unknown, untried amateur' not only shows a willingness to take risks, but also a shrewd ability to recognise talent.

At the same time, Max has a kind heart and is not averse to doing a favour for a friend. If anything, he tries to please everybody. He agrees to give Eve a job in order to satisfy Margo and, later, makes Eve Margo's understudy when Karen intervenes on her young friend's behalf. However, Max neglects to tell Margo of the new arrangement – probably because he is not confident of her response – prompting her accusation that he is a 'sly puss'.

Birdie Coonan (Thelma Ritter)

Key quotes

'I haven't got a union – I'm slave labour.'

'You want an argument or an answer?'

Birdie is Margo's long-time friend and companion. She has a theatrical background of her own, having played successfully in vaudeville, and until Eve's arrival it is Birdie who acts as Margo's dresser, maid and general dogsbody. She is tireless and fiercely loyal to Margo.

Birdie is tough and cynical, with a wealth of common sense and shrewd, honest instincts. Listening to Eve's tale of woe in Margo's dressing room, Birdie irreverently responds, 'What a story – everything but the bloodhounds snapping at her rear end'. In other words, Eve's account is melodramatic and far-fetched. At the same time, given that the others are clearly taken in, Birdie is good-hearted enough to appreciate that she is outnumbered and apologises to Eve.

Birdie has a low tolerance for Margo's grandstanding. The two bicker without rancour and, ultimately, Margo values what Birdie has to say. Birdie is suspicious of Eve from the start, disliking how Eve has been 'studying' Margo. Birdie makes the important distinction between Eve thinking *of* Margo and thinking *about* her, implying self-interest on Eve's part. Time proves her correct.

Claudia Casswell (Marilyn Monroe)

Key quotes

'A graduate of the Copacabana school of dramatic art.' (Addison)

'She looks like she might burn down a plantation.' (Margo)

As played by Marilyn Monroe in one of her first screen roles, Claudia is the classic blonde bombshell. She arrives at Margo's party, on the arm of her mentor Addison DeWitt, in a glamorous evening gown calculated to make an impression. Addison's reference to the Copacabana, a famous New York City nightclub, implies that Claudia's theatrical experience has been confined to a chorus line. It might also be assumed that she is a graduate of the 'casting couch' school of drama. Her weary question to Addison when he points her in the direction of Max Fabian – 'Why do they always look like unhappy rabbits?' – reveals she has been down this path before.

Claudia makes an interesting contrast to Eve and the two are explicitly compared at Claudia's audition. Although Claudia has many obvious physical assets, she has little of Eve's natural aptitude for the stage and is completely overshadowed. Nevertheless, like Eve, Claudia is prepared to do whatever it takes in order to gain an entree into the business. After the abortive audition for *Aged in Wood*, Addison continues to micro-manage her career, suggesting that her next move be into television.

Phoebe (Barbara Bates)

Key quotes

'I call myself Phoebe.'

'I don't care if I never get home.'

Phoebe's brief appearance at the end of the film is designed to underline the film's moral message. Phoebe is a younger, less subtle version of Eve: she is an ambitious young woman who fantasises about stardom, and who decides that the quickest route to fame is to attach herself to her idol. She brazenly sneaks into Eve's apartment and works quickly to establish her usefulness.

Phoebe's flirtatious manner towards Addison suggests that she will cultivate any relationship that might prove useful. In turn, Addison recognises, from the reverent way in which Phoebe handles the Siddons award, that 'more than anything else in the world', she, too, would like the acclaim it represents. His advice – 'Then you must ask Miss Harrington how to get one' – neatly acknowledges both Eve's mastery and Phoebe's desire for self-aggrandisement.

THEMES, IDEAS & VALUES

Women's roles

Key quotes

'And in the last analysis, nothing's any good unless you can look up just before dinner, or turn around in bed, and there he is. Without that, you're not a woman.' (Margo)

'To be a good actor or actress or anything else in the theatre means wanting to be that more than anything else in the world.' (Bill)

The theatrical world was one of the few contexts in the 1950s where women had independent careers. Nevertheless, the theatre was a microcosm, reflective of the values of the wider world, and the roles assumed by the men in the text signal the essentially patriarchal nature of postwar American society. There are successful actresses like Margo Channing, but it is men who hold positions of authority and influence. There are male producers, male directors and male playwrights. In Hollywood, actresses who work in film are strictly contracted to the studio system that is, of course, headed by men.

The relationship between Addison and Claudia typifies the power dynamic between men and women in the theatre. As an influential critic, Addison has the wherewithal to make or break careers and, to a hopeful young starlet like Claudia, his patronage is invaluable. Similarly, despite Eve's undeniable talent, she still sees it as professionally advantageous to form a relationship with a prominent, male high-flyer, such as Bill or Lloyd, and she cannot afford to alienate someone as powerful as Addison. The implication here is that, in an intensely competitive workplace where women are systemically disadvantaged, talent alone may not be enough.

All About Eve endorses a societal approval of marriage and its status as a romantic ideal. The text polarises the options presented to women, suggesting that they must choose between a happy marriage and a lonely career. Once having gained the former, the latter becomes expendable and women surrender a professional life. Lloyd and Karen Richards exemplify the conventional roles of male breadwinner and supportive female spouse. That Karen went to Radcliffe suggests both brains and privilege – it was rare for women of Karen's generation to go to college and even rarer to attend the prestigious sister school of Harvard University. However, like most of her peers, Karen has not pursued an independent career and relies on her husband for financial support. Lloyd's description of his wife as 'my loyal little woman' may be meant as a compliment, but it also reflects the paternalistic values of the period.

A loving marriage, such as that shared by the Richardses, is tendered as preferable to virtually any other alternative. Lloyd and Karen's marriage is the paradigm to which Margo aspires. Margo envies the apparent security of the Richardses' relationship. Marriage has a strength and a permanence that other, more informal relationships, however loving, lack. Marriage can be threatened – as Eve's plot to steal Lloyd from Karen demonstrates – but the essential integrity of the institution remains intact. Put simply, Margo believes the cultural myth that marriage offers a greater guarantee of happiness and fulfilment. Despite her fame and the professional esteem in which she is held, she believes that nothing surpasses being Bill's wife: 'I've finally got a life to live'.

By contrast, Eve is aberrant. Her promiscuity contrasts unfavourably with Karen's fidelity and even Margo's serial monogamy. Eve's predatory behaviour endangers the harmony of two happy unions. In her willingness to move from man to man in search of a partner who will further her prospects, Eve is the archetypal 'Other Woman'. Her role is to destabilise. In this sense, Eve challenges the values promoted by her society. Rather than searching for a union based on romantic love and mutual respect, Eve's quest is neither romantic nor respectful; it is blatantly opportunistic.

All About Eve also explores the issue of ageing for women. Society's undue regard for youth and beauty is even more problematic in the theatre, where a woman's face is her fortune and her capacity to credibly play many parts is limited by time. Again, a societal standard that disadvantages women compared to men comes into play. In the 1950s – and beyond – Hollywood was still offering male actors romantic leads well into their sixties, whereas actresses of forty often struggled to secure reasonable roles. The film demonstrates that there will always be a hungry young candidate waiting in the wings.

Margo is painfully conscious of the fact that she is forty and, arguably, too old for many of the roles she plays. Her age makes her vulnerable – another reason to yearn for the ostensible protection of marriage. The choice between marriage and career is exemplified by the prize role of Cora. Here, though, Margo can be sanguine about relinquishing the opportunity, knowing that she has Bill's love: 'I don't have to play parts I'm too old for, just because I've got nothing to do with my nights'.

Key point

Women are constrained by the traditional gender expectations and prejudices of the period. In a society that celebrates marriage, conflict can arise between women's independence and their need for love.

Ambition

Key quotes

'And tomorrow morning you will have won your beachhead on the shores of immortality.' (Addison)

'There never was, and there never will be, another like you!' (Addison)

Achievement in the theatre is hard-won, requiring a fearless will to succeed, as well as an unlimited capacity for hard work. Bill talks of the 'concentration of desire or ambition and sacrifice such as no other profession demands' and argues that 'the man or woman who accepts those terms can't be ordinary, can't be – just someone.' Most people in the theatrical world give too much of themselves for too little reward and those who do succeed suffer unexpected losses.

Ambition and gender

Ambition – at least in women – is presented as a damaging quality, capable of destroying relationships and corroding values. In a further example of the conservative double standard of the 1950s, women in the text are punished for their ambition in a way that men are not. It is acceptable for men like Bill or Lloyd to be ambitious and seek ways to further their career; they have women to support them and nurture their talents. Addison describes his own ambition as 'insatiable' and he and Eve are portrayed as two of a kind, both sharing a well-honed 'killer's' instinct. Yet Addison is not called to account in the same way that Eve is, rather emerging from the drama with his power and ego intact.

Dangers of ambition

All About Eve highlights the seductive pitfalls of fame. Margo has been in the limelight long enough to know that fame is a double-edged sword. She is dismissive of her fans, viewing them as 'autograph fiends' and 'coyotes'. While their presence is a measure of her success, she resents the constant attention which makes her feel like public property: 'So many people know me'. She is also at a point in her life when she can look back on her career and question the compromises she has had to make. For ambitious women, a successful career comes at a price; loss of femininity is one unspoken casualty. Margo confides to Karen that a woman's career is a 'funny business'. She mourns 'the things you drop on your way up the ladder so you can move faster. You forget you'll need them again when you get back to being a woman.'

For women, the emotional cost of negotiating a relationship and a career is challenging at best, impossible at worst. Margo's 'not a woman' speech evokes Eve and her unfeeling determination to succeed. By implication, Eve is not a 'real' woman. Her ambition is 'unfeminine' and, because of it, she has forfeited some vital human quality. Margo's final punchline underlines Eve's moral shortfall: 'I wouldn't worry too much about your heart – you can always put that award where your heart ought to be'.

However, young women like Phoebe and Claudia Casswell cannot see beyond their own passionate desire for celebrity. Phoebe's transparent jockeying for Eve's patronage signals a similar trajectory to Eve's own. Likewise, in the long-established tradition of the casting couch, Claudia attaches herself to an influential man of the theatre. In exchange for her submission to his demands (which are unspecified, but by implication will involve sexual favours), Addison will take her to parties, introduce her to the right people and give her fledgling career a nudge.

Eve's ambitions

Ambition is Eve's guiding principle and will inform the direction of her career. Her initial resistance towards Hollywood diminishes, for example, as her star rises. In the first conversation with Bill, where she is essentially paraphrasing Addison's column, Eve rejects the idea of Hollywood as 'real theatre'. However, she has no hesitation in selling out to celluloid at the first opportunity. Eve wants the acclaim of the general public, as opposed to the affirmation of a select few. The point is not whether Hollywood is good or bad, but rather that Eve has discarded her own stated principles in going there. Despite her saccharine promise to return to New York to claim her heart, the fact that she has packed a number of suitcases indicates her intention of staying indefinitely. Equally, the casual disregard with which Eve handles her prized award reveals that its gloss has already worn off, as new opportunities emerge to take Broadway's place.

Betrayal

Key quotes

Margo 'helped and trusted you. You paid her back by trying to take Bill away.' (Addison)

'It strikes me that Eve's disloyalty and ingratitude must be contagious.' (Karen)

The shadow and example of *Macbeth* hovers over *All About Eve*. Shakespeare's tragedy of the Scottish thane who betrays his king in the most heinous way – murdering him for his throne – is explicitly referenced twice in the text. The first is at the Sarah Siddons banquet where the elderly chairman quotes from the play; the second is when Lloyd remarks at Margo's party that 'the general atmosphere is very Macbeth-ish'. Macbeth's fatal flaw is unbridled ambition and the parallels with Eve are marked. Eve's willingness to betray those in high places who have supported her, in order to further her own ends is, similarly, her downfall. Individuals like Eve are seduced by an industry that trades in fantasies.

In a business where the defining elements are ambition and self-interest, Margo's cynical description of the theatrical world as a 'beehive' is apt. She asserts that 'we're all busy little bees, full of stings, making honey day and night', thus encapsulating both the tireless energy and the endemic lack of trust. Eve brings both of these qualities to the task of becoming a successful actress, endangering the dynamic between Margo, Karen, Bill and Lloyd with her intrusion into their lives. In Eve's desire to be a 'carbon copy' of Margo Channing, she is quite prepared to leapfrog over those who have supported her. Their goodwill is expendable and her dealings with them demonstrate a complete lack of integrity.

Eve acts as a malevolent catalyst, triggering negative responses between these four close friends. Karen's impulsive deception is out of character, but her exasperation with Margo's behaviour and, in particular, the way in which Eve is reviled for no apparent reason, convinces her that Margo 'had it coming'. However, Karen's friendship with Margo is, in turn, jeopardised when Eve threatens to expose her. The relationship between Bill and Lloyd also implodes during rehearsals of the new play. They fight 'bitterly and often' as Lloyd interferes with Bill's direction. While there is an element of professional frustration present, a large dose of personal emotion underpins this: simmering resentment on Bill's part and a misplaced protective instinct on Lloyd's, both generated by Eve.

Eve commits even greater betrayals when she attempts to seduce first Bill, then Lloyd. She targets these two men because they can offer her something. Bill is a talented director and Lloyd is considered the most talented playwright in America. Each, therefore, is in a position to advance the career of an aspiring young actress. The fact that they belong to the very women who first befriended Eve demonstrates how unscrupulous she is prepared to be.

By default, the text also illustrates the importance of loyalty in both personal and professional relationships. For many in the theatre, loyalty is a dispensable commodity; paradoxically, by many others, it is prized. The fragility of trust makes loyalty all the more valuable. Relationships, once broken, take time to mend and people in the business have long memories. Eve knows this when she threatens Karen about the consequences if her sabotage of Margo were to be made public: 'You and Lloyd: how long, even in the theatre, before people forgot what happened and trusted you again?' It is a serious enough charge to frighten Karen badly, both in terms of her own bond with Margo and her husband's reputation.

The theatre

Key quotes

'Lloyd always said that in the theatre, a lifetime was a season and a season a lifetime.' (Karen)

'We are a breed apart from the rest of humanity, we theatre folk. We are the original displaced personalities.' (Addison)

All About Eve looks knowingly at the theatrical milieu (environment) and the competing egos that are an integral part of it. The theatre is full of narcissistic personalities, inflated expectations and aggressive rivalries. According to Addison, those who work in the theatre 'all have abnormality in common'. He insists that actors are not only different, but 'their greatest attraction for the public is their complete lack of resemblance to normal human beings'. Audiences neither want, nor expect, their idols to be ordinary. It is no wonder, then, that the dramas offstage rival those performances witnessed onstage. Actors are 'larger than life' and are virtually given permission to behave without the constraints imposed on lesser mortals. In a secular society, they are deified (idolised). Margo asserts that the theatre represents 'All the religions in the world rolled into one, and we're gods and goddesses'.

The film references the competition that exists between the theatre and the movies: specifically, Broadway and Hollywood. The former is seen – at least by those who work in it – as culturally and artistically superior. The prevailing view, expressed by Eve when she first meets Bill, is that New York theatre has a legitimacy and integrity that Hollywood, with its brash commercialism, cannot match. In the opening scene, Addison approvingly notes that the Sarah Siddons Award for Distinguished Achievement is of a different calibre to such 'questionable honours' as 'those awards presented annually by that, ah, film society'. He references theatrical celebrities of the late nineteenth and early twentieth centuries – legends such as Helena Modjeska, Minnie Fiske and Richard Mansfield – who specialised in serious dramatic roles by the great playwrights. As an actress whose career has been exclusively in the theatre, Margo Channing is part of this illustrious tradition.

All About Eve demonstrates the way in which Hollywood attracts like a magnet. The lure of the big screen, with the fame and fortune it promises, is irresistible to writers, directors and actors. Even Addison concedes that the Sarah Siddons award is 'perhaps unknown' to the general public outside theatrical circles. Certainly to someone with Eve's drive, success in Hollywood represents the ultimate personal and professional triumph. Interestingly, Bill rejects the prejudice that the theatre and Hollywood are mutually exclusive. The idea of a bourgeois 'ivory green room' infuriates him and he argues that theatre should be an eclectic, inclusive art form that runs the gamut from opera to flea circus: '...wherever there's magic and make-believe and an audience, there's theatre'. The implication is that Broadway and Hollywood are very similar. Both are miniature worlds that mirror a broader context, sharing interchangeable issues and analogous personalities.

The text identifies the contradictions that underpin the theatrical world. For example, there is an ongoing tension between art and profit that characterises the majority of theatrical ventures. In the opening scene, Addison comments on the priorities of different producers. Most, like Max Fabian, simply want to 'make a buck'. To them, theatre is a business and one's reputation is only as good as the last success. Nevertheless, the long-term collaboration between Margo and Lloyd Richards indicates that it is possible to achieve a balance between artistic credibility and commercial viability. Herein lies another paradox – the collaborative nature of theatre is constantly threatened by opposing interests and personal egos. Rehearsals for *Footsteps on the Ceiling* show how easily these tensions can fester, even to the extent of threatening a production.

'Nothing is forever in the theatre – whatever it is, it's here, flares up, burns hot and it's gone.' Karen's observation reveals the ephemeral nature of life in the theatre. Passions run high and, just as quickly, cool; loyalties fluctuate and relationships can be fickle. Actors come and go, and an individual's time in the spotlight is brief. When Macbeth is quoted at the outset, describing life as 'a poor player that struts and frets his hour upon the stage', we are reminded that Eve's fame is transient. Despite the hungry energy that has been channelled into promoting her career, her 'hour upon the stage', like that of others before her, will be limited and one day her voice will be 'heard no more'. In fact, Eve's story might be summarised by Macbeth's words: the besieged monarch concludes with profound pessimism that life 'is a tale told by an idiot, full of sound and fury, signifying nothing'. This idea illustrates the pointlessness of Eve's quest for celebrity and calls into question the values that have driven it.

Key point

Mankiewicz holds a satirical mirror up to the theatre's more negative aspects, arguing strongly that the flawed assumptions of its practitioners can be damaging. At the same time, the film affectionately acknowledges the passion and creativity that make the theatre so exceptional.

Retribution

Key quotes

> 'That I should want you at all suddenly strikes me as the height of improbability – but that, in itself, is probably the reason.' (Addison)
>
> 'And you realise and you agree how completely you belong to me.' (Addison)

Eve's shallow victory exposes the flaws in the 'American Dream' (an enduring cultural tradition that contends that anything is possible for individuals who are prepared to work hard to attain their goals). Eve is a self-made woman in every respect. From the humble mediocrity of Wisconsin, she has risen – with fierce determination – to the heights of her profession. However, neither happiness nor emotional fulfilment is guaranteed. Little sympathy is generated for 'little Miss Evil' and, throughout the film, the audience is invited to condemn her behaviour and reject her, just as the key players in the drama do.

Eve encounters her nemesis in Addison: 'Is it possible, even conceivable, that you've confused me with that gang of backward children you play tricks on?' He is equally clever and equally unscrupulous. These two individuals are both prepared to sacrifice personal relationships in order to further their objectives – it matters little to Addison that Eve ultimately despises him – and they employ similar tactics of blackmail and coercion. After blackmailing Karen, Eve finds herself on the receiving end when Addison threatens to expose her own lies to the world. In each case, the blackmail is effective for the same reason. Loss of trust equals loss of credibility.

Addison's real hold over Eve is not so much the fact that she isn't who she says she is, but the sheer magnitude of Eve's deception. She has not merely changed her name – which, after all, is not unusual in the acting world – but invented an entire personal history. The most damning charge against her is her murky sexual history and the revelation that she had to be paid 500 dollars to get out of town. In this respect, Eve is a casualty of the conservative values of the day and her situation echoes that of other hapless women in film and literature. Blanche DuBois, the heroine of Tennessee Williams' *A Streetcar Named Desire* (1947), is confronted with her own lies in a similar way. Having abused the confidence of those around her so completely, Eve has no alternative except to comply with Addison's expectations; her erstwhile ally has become her controller and she is rendered powerless.

The night that Eve receives her award should be a joyous one, shared with friends and colleagues. However, she receives no endorsement from those who have been closest to her; Margo, Bill and the Richardses have closed ranks. As Eve accepts the Siddons statuette and delivers her speech, her apparent sincerity contrasts sharply with their stony expressions. The only time Eve falters is when she looks the smirking Addison in the eye. The 'happiest night' of her life is spoilt by her knowledge of the power he now holds over her. Eve's triumph is a hollow one and, rather than feeling elated, she understands how vulnerable she has made herself. After the dinner, her alienation is complete. She is offered perfunctory congratulations by her former friends and, instead of attending the party held in her honour, she goes home alone, only accepting Addison's offer of an escort with reluctance. This is a fitting outcome for a woman who has spurned friendship as expendable.

At the conclusion of the film, the timely appearance of Phoebe suggests that Eve will be confronted with the same self-interested resolve that she herself presented to Margo. The audience's first sighting of Phoebe is in Eve's mirror, suggesting that she is a figurative reflection of Eve herself. Phoebe's manner and conduct invite suspicion regarding her true motives. Like Eve, she has invented a new identity for herself and left her home town to try her luck in New York. She adopts the same ingratiating manner towards Eve that the latter adopted towards Margo, offering quickly to clean up a spilt drink and answer the door. Presumably, she will also attempt to insinuate her way into Eve's life so that the cycle is repeated. Eve may have won public acclaim but, in private, there are a number of foreboding hints as to her future.

DIFFERENT INTERPRETATIONS

Different interpretations arise from different responses to a text. Over time, a text will give rise to a wide range of responses from its audience, who may come from various social or cultural groups and live in very different places and historical periods. Responses by critics and reviewers can be published in newspapers, journals and books, both online and in print. They can also be expressed in discussions among audiences in the media, classrooms, book groups and so on.

While there is no single correct reading or interpretation of a text, it is important to understand that an interpretation is more than a personal opinion – it is the justification of a point of view on a text. To present an interpretation of a text based on your point of view, you must use a logical argument and support it with relevant evidence from the text.

Critical viewpoints

All About Eve was universally applauded at the time of its release and its critical appeal has never waned. In particular, the film has been praised for its literate, incisive screenplay. Bosley Crowther, writing for the *New York Times* in 1950, referred to 'the dazzling and devastating mockery that is brilliantly packed into this film'. Dan Schneider (2008) agrees that the dialogue 'still sparkles with wit nearly six decades on', although he does call the cinematography 'rather pedestrian'.

Inevitably, critics have focused on different aspects of the film. Sam Staggs, in his book *All About Eve,* argues that it remains the 'definitive movie about backstage life' (Staggs 2000), a view echoed by Mel Gussow when he asserts that '*All About Eve* stands as an acerbic satire on ambition and the egocentricity of those who dominate show business' (Gussow 2000). Roger Ebert (2000) hones in on the ageism that actresses face in the theatre, while Kevin Hagopian describes the film as 'the best analysis of the American success mania' since *Citizen Kane*. The film has also been called a 'woman's picture' – not in an exclusive or pejorative way – but because the three main female characters 'struggle with themselves in an eternal female contest: personal fulfilment through career achievement or through relationships' (Movie Reviews 2001).

Elements of the film have continued to intrigue critics and commentators. Staggs discusses at length the film's 'subtext' and the way in which Eve's homosexuality is encoded in the narrative. Robert J. Corber (2005) draws an interesting correlation between the way in which gays and lesbians were depicted under the Production Code and the political context. He suggests that while Eve is 'one of a long line of predatory celluloid lesbians in Code-era films', her 'impersonation of normative femininity' parallels the supposed infiltration of communists into American society and the threat they were seen to present.

Two interpretations of *All About Eve*

Interpretation 1: *All About Eve* shows how difficult it is to maintain close relationships in the theatre.

In *All About Eve*, the theatre is described as a 'big stone jungle', a 'beehive' and a 'rat-race'. These unflattering descriptions suggest a professional climate that is far from conducive to establishing and maintaining close relationships. The intense competition to succeed means that it is usually a case of 'every man for himself'.

The theatre is an opportunistic environment at best. Even those who consider themselves good friends tend to favour what is most expedient. For example, as well as enjoying a professional relationship, Max Fabian is a welcome guest in Margo's house and they are clearly fond of each other. Furthermore, Max is a benign and accommodating individual who is happy to do his friends a favour. Yet even he is not entirely trustworthy, as he goes behind Margo's back to appoint Eve as her understudy without telling her. Nor does their long friendship prevent them from screaming at each other, with Max threatening to bring in lawyers if Margo breaks her contract. Experience has taught Margo to trust few people. She draws a sour distinction between the theatre and 'civilisation', saying that in the theatre, 'everybody's guilty till they're proved innocent'.

Ambition is so ubiquitous in the theatre that relationships are often reduced to transactions. Eve cultivates Karen's friendship precisely because the latter can be of use to her. Karen's genuine and well-meaning offer of friendship is exploited and provides Eve with the contacts that she needs. Eve keeps milking this relationship for as long as she is able: 'I'm about to ask you for another favour – after all you've done already'. Later, when Eve blackmails Karen, she insultingly describes the incident as 'a simple exchange of favours'. Even more blatant is the 'exchange of favours' a young starlet like Claudia Casswell is prepared to make in order to get her foot in the theatrical door. Having seemingly slept with Addison DeWitt, she then follows Addison's directive to 'Go and do yourself some good' by targeting Max, who does, in fact, reward her attentions by giving her an audition.

The text demonstrates that every relationship is vulnerable. A close friendship like Bill and Lloyd's can still be compromised by professional differences and personal tensions. The hostility generated between them during preparations for the new play alarms Karen enough for her to eschew her usual practice of attending the rehearsals. Her own, ostensibly secure, marriage is also threatened by Eve – hardly an aberrant occurrence in an industry where actors, directors and playwrights work in close proximity to young, attractive actresses. In reality, Eve admits to Addison that her interest in Lloyd is purely strategic. She is working on the 'perfect' supposition that the relationship will further her own career: 'There's no telling how far we can go ... he'll write great plays for me; I'll make them great'.

In the theatre, romantic relationships can be short-lived and are continually under threat. Again, the temptations that accompany difficult working hours and an itinerant lifestyle are considerable. Margo lives in constant fear that she will lose Bill to 'some wide-eyed young babe'. When Karen is trying to reassure Margo that Bill loves her and the relationship is a special one, Margo gloomily retaliates with 'Isn't that what they always say?'

Eve's description of her 'friends in the theatre' – the very people she hurts and betrays – ironically highlights how shallow and ephemeral relationships can be. Events in the film illustrate clearly the pervasive lack of trust and the self-serving mentality that exemplify the industry. Addison's admitted contempt for his fellow human beings may be at the extreme end of the spectrum, but his attitude is also a cynical response to a lifetime spent observing relationships in the theatre.

Interpretation 2: *All About Eve* illustrates the genuine, distinctive bond that exists between people in the theatre.

All About Eve argues that the exacting demands imposed by the theatre produce a 'breed apart'. The work these individuals do, the hours they keep and the dreams they share spawn a sense of empathy and genuine fellowship. In spite of, or perhaps because of, the intrinsic pressures placed upon them, there is a particular bond generated among people in the theatre.

The theatre is a jealous mistress and the text suggests, by omission, that there is little opportunity to form close relationships outside the theatrical orbit. In particular, the film showcases close relationships between women in the theatre. Margo's relationship with Birdie, her 'good friend and companion', is of a long standing. Birdie's deadpan delivery can defuse Margo's black moods and brings out Margo's own sense of humour. The two friends are often shown laughing together and, whether the joke is about the difficulties of acting in a girdle or the guests at Margo's party, these women share a mutual appreciation of life's quirks. Similarly, Margo and Karen enjoy a very close bond. Karen is not overawed by the actress's fame – if anything, Margo shows more insecurity about her own less privileged background. While Karen is not prepared to indulge Margo's tantrums, she can tolerate them, explaining to Margo that she and Lloyd are never 'deeply angry' with her. Karen is also the first to defend Margo when she feels her friend is under attack. It is probably no coincidence that neither Birdie nor Karen present direct professional competition to Margo, but this does not detract from the worth of their respective friendships.

By contrast, Margo and Karen's partners, Bill and Lloyd, *have* regularly worked together. Independent of their professional collaborations, they are also good friends and the two couples socialise regularly. When Margo and Bill decide to get married, their first instinct is to share their joy with Karen and Lloyd: 'our nearest and dearest friends'. Lloyd's toast expresses the sincere affection and depth of feeling between them: 'To each of us and all of us. Never have we been more close – may we never be farther apart'. These relationships are extremely important to all concerned. They have a proven track record and are demonstrably able to withstand adversity. Margo tells Karen that, 'More than any two people I know, I don't want you and Lloyd to be angry with me'.

Margo, Bill, Karen and Lloyd are all tested by Eve's destructive interference in their lives. Despite this, their loyalty to each other remains strong. Margo's 'backwards' rendition of a line from Shakespeare's *Julius Caesar* highlights the quartet's enduring bond, as well as their renewed appreciation of the value of friendship. Shakespeare's quotation asserts that: 'The evil that men do lives after them; the good is oft interred with their bones'. Instead, in Margo's version, it is good that persists.

All About Eve suggests that the theatrical fraternity is a close-knit one. Margo's loyalty, in turn, inspires loyalty. Her friends and colleagues display this after Addison's provocative review of Eve's understudy performance. The young actress informs Karen that Broadway's sympathy is entirely with Margo: 'I've been told off in no uncertain terms all over town'. At the same time, the theatre is not necessarily depicted as an exclusive world, just an insular one. The generosity and goodwill that Karen and Margo initially show towards Eve demonstrate their readiness to embrace an outsider.

Although the text recognises the pressures produced by the theatre and the way in which such constraints can impact on relationships, it also emphasises the special connection shared by those who work in this setting. The final word on the subject belongs to Max, when he feelingly expresses the sentiment, 'It's friends that count'.

QUESTIONS & ANSWERS

This section focuses on your own analytical writing on the text, and gives you strategies for producing high-quality responses in your coursework and exam essays.

Essay writing – an overview

An essay on a literary work or a film is a formal and serious piece of writing that presents your point of view on the text, usually in response to a given topic. Your 'point of view' in an essay is your interpretation of the meaning of the text's language, structure, characters, situations and events, supported by detailed analysis of textual evidence.

Analyse – don't summarise

In your essays it is important to avoid simply summarising what happens in a text.

- A summary is a description or paraphrase (retelling in different words) of the characters and events. For example: 'Macbeth has a horrifying vision of a dagger dripping with blood before he goes to murder King Duncan.'
- An analysis is an explanation of the real meaning or significance that lies 'beneath' the text's words (and images, for a film). For example: 'Macbeth's vision of a bloody dagger shows how deeply uneasy he is about the violent act he is contemplating – as well as his sense that supernatural forces are impelling him to act.'

A limited amount of summary is sometimes necessary to let your reader know which part of the text you wish to discuss. However, always keep this to a minimum and follow it immediately with your analysis of what this part of the text is really telling us.

Plan your essay

Carefully plan your essay so that you have a clear idea of what you are going to say. The plan ensures that your ideas flow logically, that your argument remains consistent and that you stay on the topic. An essay plan should be a list of brief dot points – no more than half a page.

- Include your central argument or main contention – a concise statement (usually in a single sentence) of your overall response to the topic. See 'Analysing a sample topic' (pp.70–73) for guidelines on how to formulate a main contention.
- Write three or four dot points for each paragraph indicating the main idea and evidence/examples from the text. Note that in your essay you will need to *expand* on these points and *analyse* the evidence.

Structure your essay

An essay is a complete, self-contained piece of writing. It has a clear beginning (the introduction), middle (several body paragraphs) and end (the last paragraph or conclusion). It must also have a central argument that runs throughout, linking each paragraph to form a coherent whole.

See examples of introductions and conclusions in the 'Analysing a sample topic' (pp.70–73) and 'Sample answer' (pp.73–75) sections.

The introduction establishes your overall response to the topic. It includes your main contention and outlines the main evidence you will refer to in the course of the essay. Write your introduction *after* you have done a plan and *before* you write the rest of the essay.

The body paragraphs argue your case – they present evidence from the text and explain how this evidence supports your argument. Each body paragraph needs:

- **a strong topic sentence** (usually the first sentence) that states the main point being made in the paragraph
- **evidence** from the text, including some brief quotations
- **analysis** of the textual evidence explaining its significance and **explanation** of how it supports your argument
- **links back to the topic** in one or more statements, usually towards the end of the paragraph.

Connect the body paragraphs so that your discussion flows smoothly. Use some linking words and phrases like 'similarly' and 'on the other hand', though don't start every paragraph like this. Another strategy is to use a significant word from the last sentence of one paragraph in the first sentence of the next.

Use key terms from the topic – or synonyms for them – throughout, so the relevance of your discussion to the topic is always clear.

The conclusion ties everything together and finishes the essay. It includes strong statements that emphasise your central argument and provide a clear response to the topic.

Avoid simply restating the points made earlier in the essay – this will end on a very flat note and imply that you have run out of ideas and vocabulary. The conclusion is meant to be a logical extension of what you have written, not just a repetition or summary. Writing an effective conclusion can be a challenge. Try using these tips:

- Start by linking back to the final sentence of the second-last paragraph – this helps your writing to 'flow', rather than leaping back to your main contention straight away.
- Use synonyms and expressions with equivalent meanings to vary your vocabulary. This allows you to reinforce your line of argument without being repetitive.
- When planning your essay, think of one or two broad statements or observations about the text's wider meaning. These should be related to the topic and your overall argument. Keep them for the conclusion, since they will give you something 'new' to say but still follow logically from your discussion. The introduction will be focused on the topic, but the conclusion can present a wider view of the text.

Essay topics

1. "I'm just the carbon copy you read when you can't find the original." Is this an accurate appraisal of Eve Harrington?
2. '*All About Eve* demonstrates that women must make difficult choices if they are to have successful careers.' Discuss.

3 When confronted with Eve's dishonesty, the other characters in the film learn a great deal about themselves. Do you agree?

4 How does the film-maker encourage us to empathise with Margo Channing in spite of her flaws?

5 'In order to succeed in the theatre, the only values that count are egotism and ruthless ambition.' Is this true?

6 "... you can always put that award where your heart ought to be." Is Eve really punished for her misdeeds?

7 How does the film's multi-voiced narration contribute to our understanding of characters and events?

8 "No more make-believe, off stage or on."
'For the characters in this text, make-believe is more important than the truth.' Discuss.

9 'The women in *All About Eve* are either callous or foolish.'
Do you agree?

10 How do we learn 'all about Eve'?

Vocabulary for writing on *All About Eve*

Cinematography: the art of using the camera to capture images on film.

Circular structure: the narrative begins and ends at the same, or a similar, point in time.

Cross-cutting: the film is cut between two scenes or two events occurring simultaneously in the narrative.

Dissolve: a scene that is ending briefly overlaps or 'dissolves' into the next one.

Fade-out: an editing technique enabling a scene to dissolve into black.

Flashback / flashforward: an editing technique that shows events from the narrative's past or, alternatively, moves the plot forward to a point in the future.

Freeze-frame: an image that is frozen or 'paused'.

Intertextuality: the deliberate referencing of other texts – either by direct allusion and quotation, or indirectly by paraphrase or imitation – within a text.

Mise en scène: a French term meaning 'scene setting'. Refers to the visual and design elements of a film – actors, locations, sets, background details, costumes and lighting – and how these are assembled together.

Motif: a recurring image, object or notion used to link ideas and reinforce themes; motifs can add cohesion and unity to a text.

Multi-voiced narration: narration of a text by more than one character.

Retrospective narrative: the narrator looks back on past events – this affords them the advantage of hindsight and invites reflection on these previous experiences.

Analysing a sample topic

"I'm just the carbon copy you read when you can't find the original." Is this an accurate appraisal of Eve Harrington?

This question asks you to evaluate Eve's character, using her own claim as the springboard for your discussion. It also invites a comparison between Eve and Margo. You are asked a direct question here – you must answer it! Make your contention (whether you agree or disagree with the statement) clear in the introduction and indicate your line of argument.

- Look at the context in which the quotation appears. Why does Eve say this? Does she mean it? What does it suggest about her motives and her mood at this point? Do not take the statement at face value.
- Examine the relationship between Eve and Margo. Why does Eve imitate Margo? How deliberate is it? What is the significance?
- Consider the implications of the terms 'carbon copy' and 'original'. The underlying assumption here is that copies are always inferior. Is this true? How are Margo and Eve similar? How are they different?
- When Eve describes herself in this way, 'Eve Harrington' is still a work in progress. Look across the text and make sure you acknowledge the consequences of Eve's choices. What are her achievements? What are her losses?

The following plan is only *one* way to tackle the topic. You could certainly present a different argument: for example, emphasising the similarities between the two women, rather than the differences.

Sample introduction

In his backstage drama, *All About Eve*, Joseph Mankiewicz examines the complex dynamic between two actresses whose relationship increasingly shifts from friendship to rivalry. Eve Harrington's statement here suggests that her own acting ability is second-rate in comparison to Margo Channing's. Therefore, Eve portrays herself as a mere substitute for an actress who, by general consensus, is considered 'great'. However, Eve's disingenuous disclaimer oversimplifies a complex equation and is far from the truth. Eve is a rare talent in her own right and her star rises exponentially as the narrative unfolds. Moreover, any similarities to Margo that may exist in a professional context cease outside the theatre. Despite Eve's professed admiration for the older woman, her own values and perspective are very different. To call Eve a 'carbon copy' of Margo is not an accurate appraisal.

Body paragraph outline

Paragraph 1: Eve initially models herself on Margo – she begins by studying Margo's life as though it were a 'set of blueprints'.

- Eve is young and inexperienced; she gains her foothold in the theatre through the association with Margo and is smart enough to realise how much she can learn from the relationship.
- Birdie observes the way in which Eve 'studies' Margo, but correctly surmises that this says more about Eve's ambition than genuine regard for the older actress.
- Note the *mise en scène* and the way in which costume is used – Eve wearing Margo's old suit signals her attempts to reinforce the connection with Margo.
- Similarly, when Eve acts as Margo's understudy in *Aged in Wood*, she stays in Margo's costume in order to attract Margo's lover – presumably to remind Bill that she is a younger, more desirable version of Margo herself.

Paragraph 2: Nevertheless, Eve is a talented and exciting young actress who rapidly outgrows the role of Margo's 'understudy'.

- Addison DeWitt has a trained eye and his reaction to Eve's 'brilliant, vivid' reading indicates that she is an outstanding talent.

- Within less than a year, Eve has established herself on the Broadway stage, won the 'highest honour the theatre knows', and has been offered a film role.
- By the time Eve becomes the youngest ever winner of the Sarah Siddons Award, she has emerged from Margo's professional shadow. Note the low-angle shot as she accepts her prize.
- Furthermore, while all the indications are that Eve's career will be impressive, it will take a different direction to Margo's. Despite her early reservations, Eve has no hesitation in making the transition to Hollywood.

Paragraph 3: Outside acting, Eve's metaphor of a 'carbon copy' becomes spurious, for the simple reason that she is too different from Margo.

- Eve's moral inferiority to Margo is highlighted throughout the film. Margo values honesty, friendship and love. None of these things are important to Eve.
- Given the choice between personal relationships and personal gain, Eve unhesitatingly chooses the latter, and becomes a victim of her own self-interest.
- Margo makes the opposite choice when she turns down the role of Cora in order to be with Bill.
- At the Siddons ceremony, Margo is surrounded by close friends and her future husband – Eve's only companion is Addison, whom she despises. She goes home alone.

Sample conclusion

Throughout the text, Mankiewicz draws both overt and implied comparisons between Eve and Margo. Eve's description of herself as an inferior copy of Margo Channing actually does neither woman justice. Eve is a far better actress than she gives herself credit for and she quickly makes her mark on Broadway. Conversely, off stage, the differences between her and Margo are such that Eve could not be said to copy Margo at all – however much she might welcome or solicit the comparison. The text demonstrates that these women have different priorities and make very different choices. They are each unique individuals, neither one a replica of the other.

SAMPLE ANSWER

"No more make-believe, off stage or on."
'For the characters in this text, make-believe is more important than the truth.' Discuss.

For some of the characters in Joseph's Mankiewicz's drama, *All About Eve*, make-believe is more important than truth. They are blinded by their own vanity and self-interest and cannot see beyond their immediate aspirations. They are encouraged in this by the context of the theatre – a world that trades in dreams and illusions – where the line between pretence and the truth can be blurred. Eve herself is the primary proponent of this belief. However, the majority of the characters in this text do value honesty, both in their personal and professional lives. They are ultimately – like Margo Channing when she declares 'No more make-believe' – able to reject make-believe in favour of truth.

Make-believe underpins the theatrical world, and individuals who work in the theatre are in the business of creating fantasies. This is exemplified in the text by the central motif of the stage. Onstage, actors take on roles, dressing up and acting out stories, presenting an illusion to an audience willing to suspend disbelief for several hours. Backstage is where reality takes over. As soon as Margo comes off stage, she sheds the Southern belle crinoline that she wears for the *Aged in Wood* role. In her dressing room, she is out of costume and removing her make-up. Not all can, or choose to, make the transition so easily. After Eve gives her one performance in the same play, she stays in costume (a reminder that she is still playing a 'character') when she tries to seduce Bill Sampson. Ironically, she challenges him to search for 'truth' offstage, in the same way that he pursues it in a professional capacity. His immediate response is to tell Eve that her make-up's 'a little heavy', suggesting she is too unsubtle, or perhaps deceptive.

Stardom is a compelling fantasy. Being a successful actress is something that Eve has dreamt about for a long time – she probably is telling the truth when she describes to Margo and the Richardses the way in which 'acting and make-believe' dominated her youthful imagination. Eve is able to make the fantasy into a reality because her ambition is backed by talent. Arguably, she does understand the complexity of breaking into an industry that is fiercely competitive and has a high attrition rate. But Eve believes so passionately in her own ability to shape events that she miscalculates reality. Her ego prevents her from recognising the danger posed by Addison DeWitt and, as a result, she has to suffer his unwelcome intervention in her life. Mankiewicz's framing of the final scene, where Phoebe's image is replicated in Eve's mirror as she imagines herself winning an award, emphasises the prevalence of Eve's dreams. Thousands of girls similarly believe in 'make-believe'.

Eve's manipulation of the truth is so convincing that, initially, the characters who try to help and support her are gulled by the deception. Nevertheless, these individuals do finally recognise the truth, precisely because it is important to them. With the possible exception of Max Fabian, those who deal closely with the young actress learn 'all about Eve'. Close-ups of Margo, Bill, Karen and Lloyd at the Sarah Siddons ceremony reveal collective disenchantment on the part of the four friends – each of whom have cause to regret the association with Eve. While many will take Eve on face value, the film's flashback narration allows the audience access to the truth as it unfolds retrospectively from three informed perspectives.

When Margo tells her friends that she is no longer settling for make-believe, either off stage or on, it signifies a new phase in her life: one where she will be 'a foursquare, upright, downright, forthright married lady'. The text recognises that romantic love, in itself, can be an illusion and Margo is certainly aware of the gamble. Yet it is one she decides to take, after being convinced of the integrity of her relationship with Bill. As an actor, Margo is always striving for truth on stage; this is the key reason she is increasingly uncomfortable about taking on roles that no longer suit her years. Margo's fundamental honesty is set up in direct contrast to Eve's duplicity. Whereas Eve recoils from hearing the truth about herself, Margo intuitively surrounds herself with people, like Birdie, Bill and Karen, who value candour and are prepared to speak out honestly.

To a certain extent, all those who work in the theatre believe in its 'magic and make-believe'. Consequently, some of the characters in the text have significant difficulty even identifying the truth – at least at first. They are dazzled by the mystique of pretence. At the same time, theatre, like all art, is predicated on a fundamental paradox: it is 'a lie that tells the truth'. Bill insists that behind the artifice are hardworking professionals who endeavour to recreate a truthful vision, and that survival in the industry depends upon honest 'sweat, application and craftsmanship'. For most, therefore, truth is the critical element. Even Eve discovers that, while a passion for make-believe might be the catalyst to a life on the stage, it is difficult to sustain any illusion indefinitely.

REFERENCES & READING

Text

All About Eve 1950, dir. Joseph L. Mankiewicz, Twentieth Century Fox. Starring Bette Davis and Anne Baxter.

Websites

Corber, Robert J. 2005, 'Cold War Femme: Lesbian Visibility in Joseph L. Mankiewicz's *All About Eve*', Project Muse, http://muse.jhu.edu/journals/journal_of_lesbian_and_gay_studies/summary/v011/11.1corber.html

Crowther, Bosley 1950, '*All About Eve*; The Screen in Review', *New York Times*, 14 October, www.nytimes.com/movie/review?res=9A0CE1DB1738E73ABC4C52DFB667838B649EDE

Ebert, Roger 2000, *All About Eve*, www.rogerebert.com/reviews/great-movie-all-about-eve-1950

Gussow, Mel 2000, 'The Lasting Allure of *All About Eve*', *New York Times*, 1 October, www.nytimes.com/2000/10/01/movies/film-the-lasting-allure-of-all-about-eve.html

Hagopian, Kevin, *All About Eve*, New York State Writers Institute, www.albany.edu/writers-inst/webpages4/filmnotes/fns00n1.html

Mankiewicz, Joseph L. 1950, *All About Eve* script, Internet Movie Script Database, www.imsdb.com/scripts/All-About-Eve.html

This digital version of the script is extremely helpful for locating scenes and quotations, but note that online scripts are often sourced from early shooting versions, or are simply transcriptions by viewers, so they may contain errors or significant differences from the film version.

'Movie Reviews' 2001, Reel Classics, http://www.reelclassics.com/Commentary/Reviews/A/all_about_eve_50.htm

'Sarah Siddons' 2013, Wikipedia, http://en.wikipedia.org/wiki/Sarah_Siddons

Schneider, Dan 2008, *All About Eve, The Spinning Image*, www.thespinningimage.co.uk/cultfilms/displaycultfilm.asp?reviewid=5217

'The Production Code of 1930', University of North Dakota, www.und.edu/instruct/cjacobs/ProductionCode.htm

Further reading

Carey, Gary 1972, *More About All About Eve*, Random House, New York.

Mankiewicz, Joseph L. 1951, *All About Eve*: *A Screenplay*, Random House, New York.

Mankiewicz, Joseph L. and Dauth, Brian (ed.) 2008, *Joseph L Mankiewicz: Interviews*, University Press of Mississippi, Mississippi.

Staggs, Sam 2000, *All About All About Eve*, St Martin's Press, New York.